£9.50

THE STORAGE OF FLAMMABLE LIQUIDS IN CONTAINERS

HSG51

HSE BOOKS

© *Crown copyright 1998*
Applications for reproduction should be made in writing to:
Copyright Unit, Her Majesty's Stationery Office, St Clements House,
2-16 Colegate, Norwich NR3 1BQ

First published 1990
Second edition 1998

ISBN 0 7176 1471 9

This guidance is issued by the Health and Safety Executive. Following the guidance is not compulsory and you are free to take other action. But if you do follow the guidance you will normally be doing enough to comply with the law. Health and safety inspectors seek to secure compliance with the law and may refer to this guidance as illustrating good practice.

CONTENTS

PREFACE

This book provides information on the fire and explosion hazards associated with the storage of flammable liquids in containers. It sets out practical measures on the design, construction, operation and maintenance of storage areas, buildings and rooms used for storing flammable liquids at normal (ie ambient) temperatures and pressures. It gives examples of storage facilities for a number of different types of business. These measures are designed to protect people at work and others who may be affected by the storage of flammable liquids.

The guidance is aimed at those directly responsible for the safe storage and handling of flammable liquids in containers in all general work activities, ranging from the storage of small quantities of flammable liquids within a workroom, to large drum storage and distribution areas at manufacturers' or suppliers' premises.

Safety specialists and trade organisations or associations may wish to use this publication as a basis for more specific guidance for their own members.

While the references to British or other standards made in this book specify their year of issue, it is recognised that they are regularly updated and many are harmonised into a common European standard. Invariably, any such replacement standards may be used in place of the standards quoted.

OBJECTIVES

The objectives for this publication are to:

(a) help in the assessment of the risks from the storage of flammable liquids in containers, and advise on how to control those risks;

(b) increase the awareness of the potential fire and explosion hazards associated with the storage of flammable liquids in containers;

(c) advise on safe management procedures and precautions to reduce injuries and damage caused by fires and explosions during the storage of flammable liquids in containers;

(d) give guidance on the appropriate standards for the design and construction of storage areas, buildings and rooms used for storing flammable liquids at ambient temperature and pressure; and

(e) advise on the need for appropriate fire precautions, maintenance, training and good housekeeping where flammable liquids are stored in containers.

The storage of flammable liquids in containers

INTRODUCTION

General

1   This book provides you with guidance on the control measures you could adopt for the safe storage of containers containing flammable liquids. It sets out the steps you need to take to control the risks of fire and explosion, although some general advice is given on health risks where this may be helpful.

2   The guidance applies to all storage locations whether in the open air, or in specifically designed buildings, rooms or cabinets. It applies to new and existing sites.

Legal requirements

3   This book will help in your assessment of the risks arising from the storage of flammable liquids in containers, and it gives advice on how to control the risks. Assessment, by employers and the self-employed, of the risks to employees and others who may be affected by the work activities is one of the requirements of the Management of Health and Safety at Work Regulations 1992[1].

4   This book also advises you on how to comply with the relevant parts of the Health and Safety at Work etc Act 1974[2] at places where flammable liquids are stored and, where applicable, with the Highly Flammable Liquids and Liquefied Petroleum Gases Regulations 1972[3] and other relevant legislation (see Appendix 1).

5   Current legislation, guidance literature and standards are referred to in the text and are listed in the references section. They are subject to amendment from time to time. You need to ensure that the requirements, at the time any work or alterations are carried out, reflect the current legal requirements and good accepted practice. The glossary at the back of this book explains the particular terms used in the text.

What is risk assessment

6   A risk assessment is an organised look at your work activities using the following five steps:

Step 1:   Look for the hazards.

Step 2:   Decide who may be harmed and how.

Step 3:   Evaluate the risks arising from the hazards and decide whether existing precautions are adequate or if more needs to be done.

Step 4:   Record your significant findings.

Step 5:   Review your assessment from time to time and revise it if necessary.

Advice on carrying out risk assessments is contained in an HSE leaflet[4].

7   The remaining sections of this book will help you to identify many of the hazards associated with the storage of flammable liquids in containers, and give guidance on how you can reduce the risks.

8   The guidance shows many of the issues you need to consider when carrying out risk assessments. It will help in deciding which precautions are necessary concerning the storage arrangements for flammable liquids in containers. A complete risk assessment made under the Management of Health and Safety at Work Regulations 1992[1] will also have to consider other hazards, for example manual handling and transport safety, which are not within the scope of this book.

Scope

Definition of flammable liquid

9   In this book 'flammable liquid' generally means a liquid with a flashpoint of 55°C or below.

10   This definition includes:

(a)   all liquids classified as flammable, highly flammable or extremely flammable for supply according to the Chemicals (Hazard, Information and Packaging for Supply) Regulations 1994 (as amended)[5]; and

(b)   highly flammable liquids as defined in the Highly Flammable Liquids and Liquefied Petroleum Gases Regulations 1972[3].

11   This definition does not include however liquids, with a flashpoint equal to or more than 21°C and less than or equal to 55°C, which do not support combustion when tested at 55°C according to the method described in Schedule 2 of the Highly Flammable Liquids and Liquefied Petroleum Gases Regulations 1972[3].

12   Some Regulations, particularly those concerned with the transport of dangerous goods, define flammable liquids as those with a flashpoint of less than or equal to 61°C. Although some of the liquids defined according to transport legislation will be outside the scope of this book, it will nevertheless still be good practice to store them according to the recommendations given here.

Applying the standards

13   The advice in this book provides you with suitable standards for the design and location of storage facilities for flammable liquids in containers. It is applicable to flammable liquids contained in metal, glass and plastic receptacles, drums, barrels, tins, IBCs (Intermediate Bulk Containers) etc.

14   It may be inappropriate or impractical for you to adopt all the recommendations in this book at existing premises. However the law requires you to make any improvements which are reasonably practicable, taking into account the risks at the premises and the cost and feasibility of additional precautions. See the Glossary for a definition of the term reasonably practicable at the back of this book.

15   This book describes a number of ways of achieving an adequate standard of safety. Further advice on how to use it at specific sites can be obtained from whoever inspects the site for health and safety, usually HSE or the local authority.

Environmental protection

16   Spillages of flammable liquids can have environmental consequences and may be subject to controls under the Environmental Protection Act 1990[6].

17   Although this guidance does not attempt to cover environmental issues, the advice it contains for safe storage conditions will generally also provide some protection for the environment. You can find information on the environmental hazards posed by a particular flammable liquid in the specific substance material safety data sheet (MSDS) available from the supplier.

18   Further guidance is available from the Environment Agency (or in Scotland, the Scottish Environment Protection Agency (SEPA)) or from local authorities, who enforce the 1990 Act[6].

Additional advice and information

19   You can find more appropriate advice in documents listed in the Further reading section at the back of this book about:

(a)   carriage, loading and unloading, spraying and use of flammable liquids;

(b)   dispensing and storage of petrol at filling stations; and

(c)   specific industries.

20   The advice in this book does not apply to the following flammable liquids:

(a)   those which present special hazards requiring specific precautions, such as:

(i)   ethylene oxide;

(ii)   peroxides;

(iii)   other liquids which carry a risk of rapid decomposition, polymerisation or spontaneous combustion;

(b)   those contained in aerosols or other pressurised containers;

(c)   liquefied petroleum gas;

(d)   other substances which are gases at ambient temperature and pressure but are stored as liquids under pressure.

21   This book does not apply to containers with capacities of greater than approximately 1000 litres. For larger containers and those which are connected directly to a process or other point of use, advice is contained in an HSE publication[7].

Liquids with a flashpoint in the range 32°C to 55°C

22   Some of the precautions and control measures are not appropriate for lower hazard liquids with a flashpoint in the range 32°C to 55°C.

23   Advice on variations for these liquids is contained in paragraphs 171-183.

24   Where no variation is shown for any aspect, the standards in the main text apply.

Flammable liquids which are pesticides

25   All pesticides are subject to Part III of the Food and Environment Protection Act 1985 (FEPA)[8], and they must be approved either:

(a)   under the Control of Pesticides Regulations 1986[9] (as amended); or

(b)   under the Plant Protection Products Regulations 1995[10] (as amended) and the Plant Protection Products (Basic Conditions) Regulations 1997[11].

The FEPA Part III Code of Practice[12] and HSE Agriculture information sheet No 16[13] are available for guidance on the safe storage of pesticides.

26   However, you may use this book for more detail on the precautions needed to deal with the flammable hazard of such pesticides.

The storage of flammable liquids in containers

HAZARDS

Main hazards

27   The main hazards from the storage of flammable liquids are fire and explosion, involving either the liquid or the vapour given off from it. Fires or explosions are likely to occur when liquid or vapour is released and comes into contact with a suitable ignition source, or alternatively, when a heat or fire source comes into contact with the container.

28   Common causes or contributory factors of such incidents include:

(a)   lack of awareness of the properties of flammable liquids;

(b)   operator error, due to lack of training;

(c)   inadequate or poor storage facilities;

(d)   hot work on or close to flammable liquid containers;

(e)   inadequate design, installation or maintenance of equipment;

(f)   decanting flammable liquids in unsuitable storage areas;

(g)   exposure to heat from a nearby fire;

(h)   dismantling or disposing of containers containing flammable liquids.

Combustion of liquids

29   Combustion of liquids occurs when flammable vapours released from the surface of the liquid ignite (see Figure 1).

FUEL
Flammable gases
Flammable liquids
Flammable solids
General combustible materials

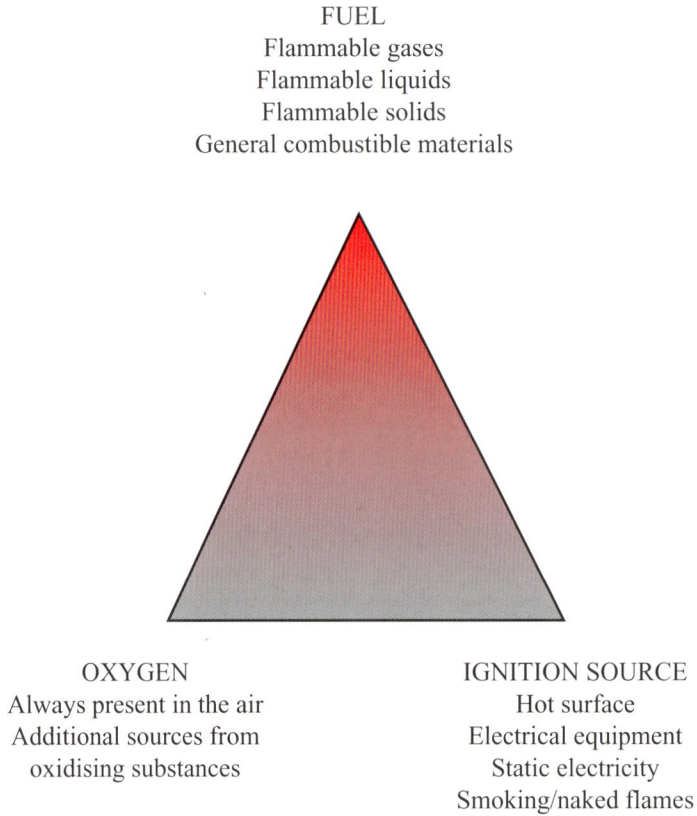

OXYGEN
Always present in the air
Additional sources from
oxidising substances

IGNITION SOURCE
Hot surface
Electrical equipment
Static electricity
Smoking/naked flames

Figure 1 The fire triangle

30   The extent of a fire or explosion hazard depends on the amount of flammable vapour given off from a liquid which is determined by:

(a)   the temperature of the liquid;

(b)   the volatility of the liquid;

(c)   how much of the surface area is exposed;

(d)   how long the liquid is exposed for; and

(e)   the air movement over the surface.

31   Other physical properties of the liquid give additional information on how vapour/air mixtures may develop and also on the potential hazards. These physical properties include:

(a)   flashpoint;

(b)   auto-ignition temperature;

(c)   viscosity;

(d)   lower explosion limit; and

(e)   upper explosion limit.

Flashpoint

32   Flashpoint is defined as the lowest temperature at which a liquid gives off vapour in sufficient quantity to form a combustible mixture with air near the surface of the liquid under specified test conditions. Generally, a liquid with a flashpoint below the ambient temperature of the surroundings will give off sufficient vapour to mix with the air and be ignited. Liquids with a flashpoint greater than ambient temperature are less likely to give off a flammable concentration of vapour unless they are heated, mixed with low flashpoint materials or released under pressure as a mist or spray. The lower the flashpoint of a liquid, the higher the risk.

Viscosity

33   The viscosity of the liquid is also significant as it determines how far any spilt material will spread and therefore the size of any exposed surface.

Health hazards

34   Flammable liquids can pose a health hazard if they are ingested, come into contact with skin or eyes, or their vapours are inhaled. For example, methanol is toxic as well as flammable. Information on the health hazards of a particular liquid, and on any specific precautions required, should be obtained from the material safety data sheet (MSDS) or from the supplier. The Control of Substances Hazardous to Health Regulations 1994[14] require employers to assess the health risks from exposure to hazardous substances and the precautions needed. Paragraphs 37-39 give further details on health precautions.

The storage of flammable liquids in containers

SAFETY PRECAUTIONS

Introduction

35   Although this book describes ways in which you can achieve an adequate standard of safety, variations from these may be appropriate to meet local conditions. You may use therefore alternative designs, materials and methods where your risk assessment shows that they provide an equivalent or higher overall level of safety.

36   The precautions outlined do not take into account possible damage from an external source such as a major incident that affects a wide area.

Health precautions

37   Many precautions for reducing fire and explosion risks will also control the health risks. But some additional measures may be necessary since concentrations of vapours, capable of damaging human health, are usually significantly below the flammable levels.

38   The Control of Substances Hazardous to Health Regulations 1994[14] require employers to prevent or control exposure to harmful substances. Guidance on these Regulations is contained in the Approved Codes of Practice (ACOPs) entitled *General COSHH ACOP, Carcinogens ACOP and Biological Agents ACOP: Control of Substances Hazardous to Health Regulations 1994*[15].

39   An obvious precaution to take against skin and eye contact is to provide items such as gloves, protective clothing and goggles. Suitable respiratory protection may be needed during any operations to deal with leaks and spillages.

Marking and labelling

40   Individual containers must be clearly marked to indicate their contents and the degree of flammability. In most cases this will be required by the Chemicals (Hazard Information and Packaging for Supply) Regulations 1994[5] (as amended) (CHIP) and the Carriage of Dangerous Goods (Classification, Packaging and Labelling) and Use of Transportable Pressure Receptacle Regulations 1996[16] (CDG(CPL)). Certain anomalies may exist with regard to the labelling of liquids with flashpoints in the range 56-61°C. For these liquids, flammability labelling is not required under CHIP, but is required under the CDG(CPL) Regulations[16].

41   The Health and Safety (Safety Signs and Signals) Regulations 1996[17] require stores and areas containing significant quantities (greater than 25 tonnes) of dangerous substances to be identified by appropriate warning signs.

42   The majority of sites on which 25 tonnes or more of dangerous substances are stored must be marked in accordance with the Dangerous Substances (Notification and Marking of Sites) Regulations 1990[18].

43   Storerooms, cupboards and bins need to be marked to indicate the hazards associated with their contents. The yellow hazard triangle symbols (see Figure 2), which are widely available, indicate the flammability hazards clearly. If it is not reasonably practicable to mark directly on the storage area, then it can be displayed nearby. 'No smoking' and 'No naked lights' notices may be appropriate.

Maintenance and modifications

44   Many incidents involving flammable liquids occur during maintenance and repairs.

Figure 2 Hazard triangle symbol

45   The likelihood is increased if the work is done by staff or outside contractors who have little knowledge of the hazards associated with flammable liquids. You should only employ experienced contractors. A guide is available which gives sound practical advice for selecting and managing contractors[19].

46   The Health and Safety at Work etc Act 1974[2] and the Management of Health and Safety at Work Regulations 1992[1] place duties to ensure safe working practices on both the company using the services and the contractor.

47   It is essential that no maintenance work is done until:

   (a)   the potential hazards of the work have been clearly identified and assessed;

   (b)   the precautions needed have been specified in detail;

   (c)   the necessary safety equipment has been provided; and

   (d)   adequate and clear instruction has been given to all those concerned.

48   In most cases, a permit-to-work (PTW) system should be used to control maintenance operations[20] in areas where flammable liquids are stored or used. PTWs are formal management documents (see Figure 3). They should only be issued by those with clearly assigned authority to do so, and the requirements stated in them must be complied with before the permit is issued and the work covered by it is undertaken. Individual PTWs need to relate to clearly defined individual pieces of work. PTWs should normally include:

   (a)   the location and nature of the work intended;

   (b)   identification of the hazards, including the residual hazards and those introduced by the work itself;

   (c)   the precautions necessary, for example, isolations;

   (d)   the personal protective equipment required;

   (e)   the proposed time and duration of the work;

   (f)   the limits of time for which the permit is valid; and

   (g)   the person in direct control of the work.

49   Further advice on PTWs is available in an HSE leaflet[21].

50   There are some simple controls you can adopt to reduce the risks of fire and explosion during maintenance hot work. You need to make sure that all flammable or combustible materials are removed from the work area. If it is not reasonably practicable to remove such materials, then you could position suitable screens or partitions to protect the hazardous inventory. Once the work has finished, you need to thoroughly inspect the area for at least an hour to ensure that there is no smouldering material present.

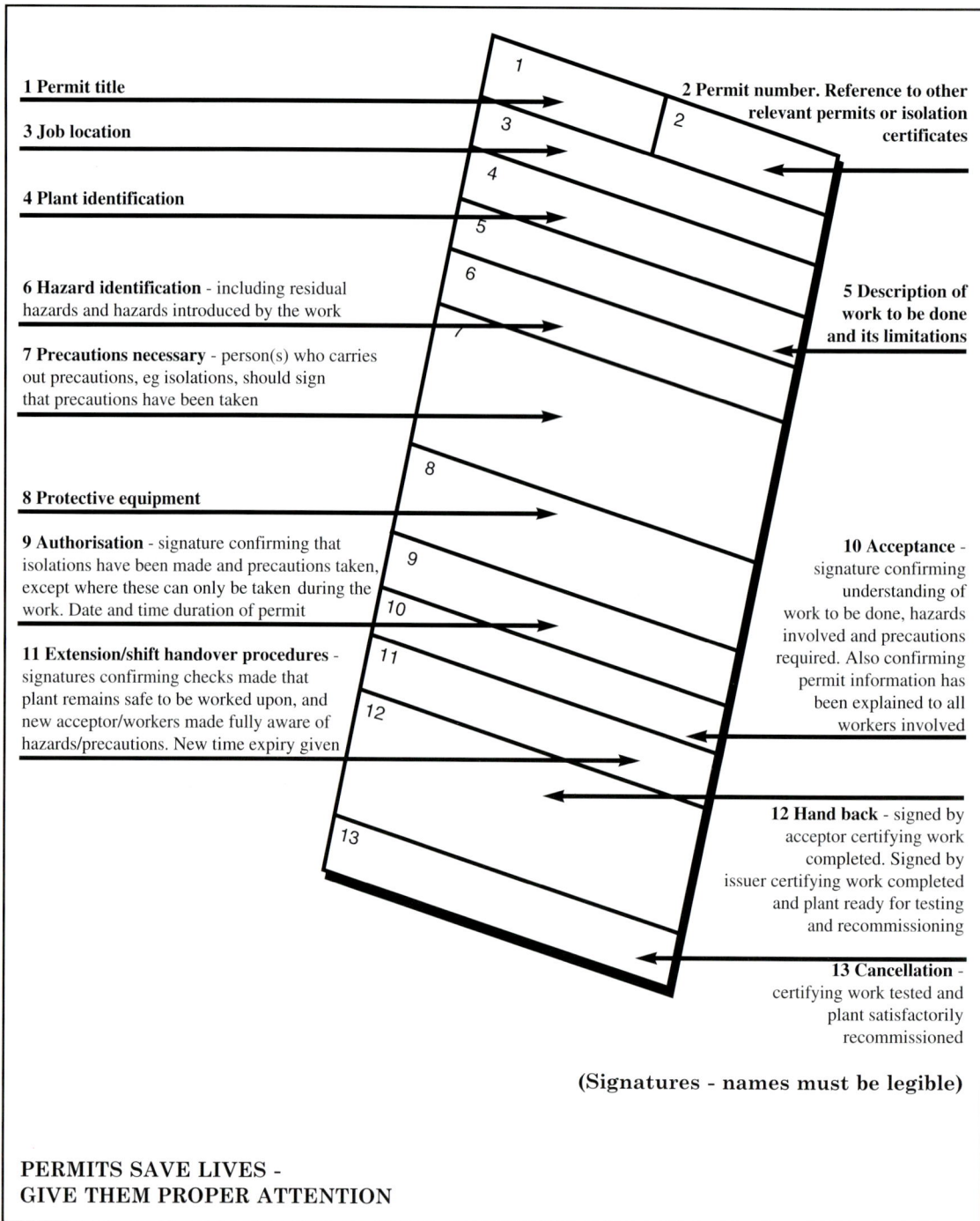

1 Permit title

3 Job location

4 Plant identification

6 Hazard identification - including residual hazards and hazards introduced by the work

7 Precautions necessary - person(s) who carries out precautions, eg isolations, should sign that precautions have been taken

8 Protective equipment

9 Authorisation - signature confirming that isolations have been made and precautions taken, except where these can only be taken during the work. Date and time duration of permit

11 Extension/shift handover procedures - signatures confirming checks made that plant remains safe to be worked upon, and new acceptor/workers made fully aware of hazards/precautions. New time expiry given

2 Permit number. Reference to other relevant permits or isolation certificates

5 Description of work to be done and its limitations

10 Acceptance - signature confirming understanding of work to be done, hazards involved and precautions required. Also confirming permit information has been explained to all workers involved

12 Hand back - signed by acceptor certifying work completed. Signed by issuer certifying work completed and plant ready for testing and recommissioning

13 Cancellation - certifying work tested and plant satisfactorily recommissioned

(Signatures - names must be legible)

PERMITS SAVE LIVES - GIVE THEM PROPER ATTENTION

Figure 3 PTW

Information and training

51   Adequate training and knowledge of the properties of flammable liquids are essential for their safe storage.

52   Training is a requirement of the Management of Health and Safety at Work Regulations 1992[1]. Carrying out risk assessments required by these Regulations will identify how much information, training and retraining are needed. Further guidance on these Regulations is contained in an Approved Code of Practice[22].

53   You need to inform all staff on the site about the hazards of storing flammable liquids, and about the need to exclude sources of ignition and heat from the designated storage areas. Those responsible for the operation of the store also need to receive specific training in how to deal with spillages and leaks, and emergency procedures.

54   Periodic retraining will normally be required. The training should include the following aspects:

(a)   the types of flammable liquid stored, their properties and hazards;

(b)   general procedures for safe handling;

(c)   use of protective clothing;

(d)   housekeeping;

(e)   reporting of faults and incidents, including minor leaks and spills; and

(f)   emergency procedures, including raising the alarm, calling the fire brigade and the use of appropriate fire-fighting equipment.

You will need written procedures for controlling the risks from the storage of flammable liquids, and these should be used as the basis for training.

The VICES principles

55   There are five general principles for ensuring that the risks of fire and explosion, from the storage of flammable liquids in containers, are controlled and minimised. An aid to remembering these five principles is the acronym 'VICES'. There is no order of priority of the principles implied by the use of the acronym.

V   **Ventilation**
Is there plenty of fresh air where containers are stored? Good ventilation means vapours given off from a spill, leak, or release, will be rapidly dispersed.

I   **Ignition**
Have all ignition sources been removed from the storage area? Ignition sources can vary widely. They include sparks from electrical equipment or welding and cutting tools, hot surfaces, smoking, and open flames from heating equipment.

C   **Containment**
Are your flammable liquids stored in suitable containers? Will a spillage be contained and prevented from spreading to other parts of the storage area or site? A means of controlling spillage would be the use of an impervious sill or low bund. An alternative is to drain the area to a safe place, such as a remote sump or a separator.

E   **Exchange**
Can you exchange a flammable liquid for a less flammable one? This is a basic question you should always ask. Can you eliminate the storage of flammable liquids from your operation altogether?

S   **Separation**
Are flammable liquids stored well away from other processes and general storage areas? Can they be separated by a physical barrier, wall or partition?

56   The remainder of this publication covers detailed control measures, essentially based on the 'VICES' principles.

Ventilation

Introduction

57   To prevent dangerous concentrations of flammable vapours building up in a store or storage area as the result of a leak, the space needs to be adequately ventilated.

58   Containers should, where reasonably practicable, be stored in the open air at ground level (singly or in stacks). This enables leaks or releases to be quickly seen, and allows for any vapours to be dispersed effectively by natural ventilation. They should not normally be stored on the roof of a building but if, for reasons of space, the use of rooftop storage is considered essential, the enforcing authority and the fire authority need to be consulted.

59   If the best option of storing containers outside is not reasonably practicable, they may be kept in suitable storerooms, preferably separate buildings specifically designed for the purpose.

Ventilation within buildings

60   You need a good standard of ventilation in buildings or rooms used for storing flammable liquids, to disperse the vapours from any small releases. The ventilation

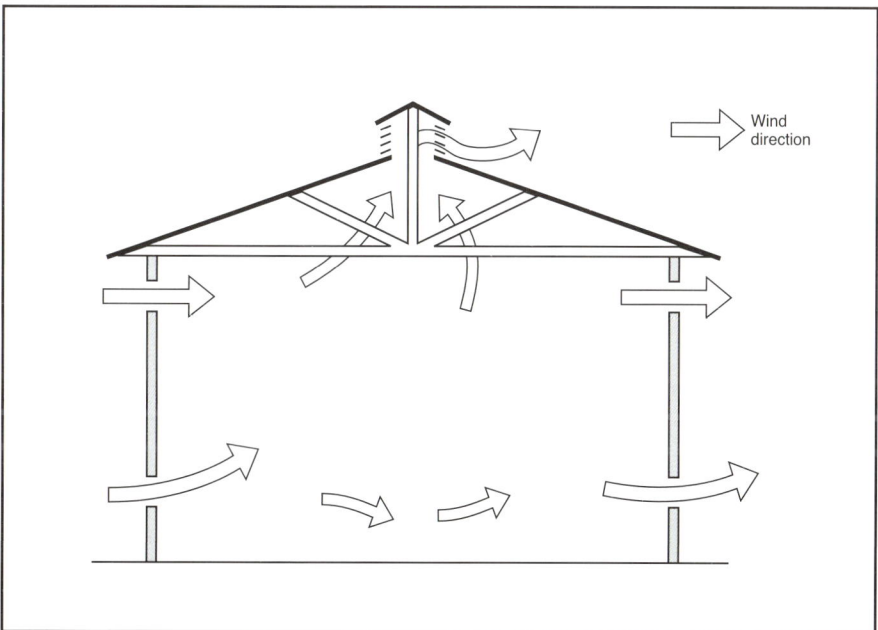

Figure 4 Roof and wall vents together give good natural ventilation

arrangements need to take into account the heavy nature of the vapours, and to ensure adequate air movement at high and low levels.

61   Five air changes per hour is normally sufficient to ensure vapour levels in the store are kept to a low level. For small buildings, the simplest method of ensuring adequate ventilation is to provide fixed, permanent openings (such as air bricks or louvers etc) at high and low levels in external walls to the outside air. The five air changes per hour may be achieved if these openings have a total area equivalent to 1-3% of the total area of the walls and roof of the store. The actual area required depends on whether the building is in exposed or sheltered weather conditions. BS 5925: 1991[23] gives advice on ventilation principles and designing for natural ventilation in buildings.

62   In cases of doubt, measurements may be taken of the air change rate actually achieved in a completed building. A competent ventilation engineer should be able to do this.

63   If openings are present on two walls, a cross-flow induced by wind forces is encouraged. Vents provided at high and low level will encourage air circulation by thermal currents (see Figure 4). Remember not to position ventilation openings in internal walls, or below the level of any containment sill provided. The openings should not be obstructed on either side by, for example, container stacks, dirt or rubbish.

64   Ventilation openings should not normally be installed in any partitions designed to be fire-resisting (see Appendix 2). Where this is unavoidable, such openings will be required to self-close in a fire situation so as to provide separation. You should seek the advice of competent fire engineers if this option is considered.

Providing mechanical ventilation

65   If the provision of natural ventilation is not possible, because, for example, the storeroom is located centrally within a large workroom, then adequate ventilation can be provided by mechanical means. Larger buildings, stores with only one or two outside walls, or buildings in sheltered locations are also likely to require mechanical ventilation.

66   Where this is provided it needs to operate constantly. Failure of an extraction system can be detected by an airflow monitoring device installed in the ductwork (such as a flow switch or differential pressure switch) and linked to an alarm.

67   Remember that the exhausted air needs to be routed to a safe place in the open air, via fire-resisting ductwork (see Appendix 2). Ducts should be arranged so that vapours cannot condense and collect at low points within the ductwork. In most cases it should be adequate if the ventilation ductwork is terminated:

(a)   at least 3 metres above ground level;

(b)   at least 3 metres from building openings, boundaries, sources of ignition; and

(c)   away from building eaves and other obstructions.

Requirements for positioning exhausts from ventilation systems may be found in Process Guidance Notes issued under the Environmental Protection Act[6].

68   Electric motors situated in the path of the vapour being extracted in ventilation ducting may become coated in flammable residues. Such residues may cause overheating of the motor and the residues themselves may undergo spontaneous combustion. Motors inside ductwork are also difficult to maintain. The Highly Flammable Liquids and Liquefied Petroleum Gases Regulations 1972[3] prohibit the positioning of electric motors (including explosion-protected motors) in ductwork containing flammable vapours.

69   You can use centrifugal or bifurcated fans, or a motor situated in a safe area can be connected to a fan by a belt drive. Remember that it is possible for slipping drive belts to generate significant heat. Fans made from non-sparking materials provide an additional precaution against friction sparks.

Ignition

70   The main objective when handling flammable liquids is always to avoid the unwanted creation of flammable concentrations of vapours by containment and ventilation. However when flammable concentrations of vapour do occur, either during normal operations or during accidental spillage etc, controls must exist over the wide variety of potential ignition sources (see Figure 5).

71   Hazardous area classification is widely used to determine the extent of hazardous zones created by flammable concentrations of vapours. Hazardous area classification is discussed further in Appendix 3.

72   The concept of hazardous area classification has, in the past, been used solely as the basis for selecting fixed electrical equipment. However, you can use it to help eliminate potential ignition sources, including portable electrical equipment, vehicles, hot surfaces etc, from flammable atmospheres.

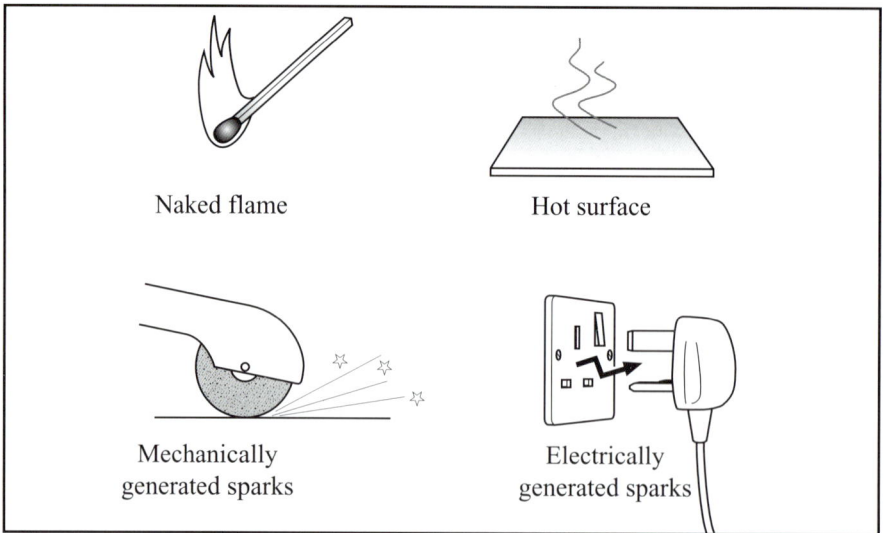

Figure 5 A range of potential ignition sources

Sources of ignition

73   Sources of ignition should be excluded from areas where flammable liquids are stored or handled. Common sources of ignition include:

(a)   naked flames, including welding and cutting equipment;

(b)   smoking;

(c)   electrical lighting, power circuits and equipment which are not suitably protected against igniting a flammable vapour, eg not flameproof or intrinsically safe;

(d)   processes or vehicles that involve friction or the generation of sparks;

(e)   hot surfaces;

(f)   static electricity.

74   Examples of controls for some ignition sources are given in the following paragraphs.

Storage of easily ignitable goods

75   Stocks of combustible materials such as easily ignitable packaging should not be kept in a flammable liquid store. These may act as the first materials to be ignited in a fire rather than the flammable liquids.

76   The fire risk will be increased if you allow combustible materials (including weed growth) to build up in a storage area, or within 1 metre of the sill or bund. If weedkillers are used, you should not use products which are oxidising agents, eg those which contain sodium chlorate, and the dead weeds need to be removed.

Electrical equipment

77   Where possible you need to locate electrical equipment in non-hazardous areas. However, if such equipment needs to be located in a hazardous environment, exposed to flammable substances, it must be constructed or protected so as to prevent danger. This is a requirement of the Electricity at Work Regulations 1989[24] and might be achieved by selecting equipment built to explosion-protected standards.

78   Advice on selecting, installing and maintaining explosion-protected electrical equipment is given in BS EN 60079-14[25] and in a short guide published by the Institution of Chemical Engineers[26].

79   There are also Regulations which apply to both electrical and non-electrical equipment, the Equipment and Protective Systems Intended for Use in Potentially Explosive Atmospheres Regulations 1996[27]. However, they are aimed at manufacturers and suppliers, requiring them to ensure the equipment is safe. Such equipment should carry CE marking. From July 2003 you will have to select such equipment but, until then, you can select equipment that does not carry CE marking provided it is safe.

Figure 6 Protected fork-lift truck

Protection of vehicles

80 Vehicles that need to operate within areas classified as hazardous zones in storage buildings or areas should be protected to an appropriate standard, to avoid ignition of flammable vapours. During storage, the highest probability of a release from a container occurs when it is being handled. An unprotected fork-lift truck may be a source of ignition in such circumstances.

81 Where only liquids with a flashpoint above 32°C are present, vehicle protection is not required unless, of course, ambient temperatures approach 32°C.

82 The HSE guidance publication HSG113[28] provides further advice on the use and protection of vehicles.

Space heating

83 Occasionally storage buildings or internal stores containing flammable liquids are heated. In this case the heating system should not be an ignition source. This can be achieved by ensuring that only indirect heating means are used. For example you could have radiators, fed remotely by hot water pipes, or indirectly fired gas or oil appliances (ie those which take the air for combustion from safe areas and exhaust the products of combustion to the outside air). Electrically heated radiators complying with BS EN 60079-14[25] may be used.

84 In all cases the heating system needs to be protected against the build-up of flammable residues on hot surfaces. The maximum temperature of any exposed heating surfaces should not exceed the auto-ignition temperature of any of the flammable liquids in storage. Guidance on this issue is contained in BS EN 60079-14[25].

Containment

Introduction

85 The main protection against the dangers arising from the storage of flammable liquids in containers is the integrity of the packaging. Individual containers may leak, break or be punctured, causing a small escape of material. You need to have arrangements in place to deal with these situations.

Design and construction of containers

86 It is a requirement of both the Chemicals (Hazard Information and Labelling for Supply) Regulations 1994 (as amended)[5] and the Carriage of Dangerous Goods (Classification, Packaging and Labelling) and Use of Transportable Pressure Receptacles Regulations 1996[16] that manufacturers, suppliers and distributors of chemicals ensure that they are packaged safely.

87 All containers should be designed and constructed to standards suitable for the purpose. They should be robust and have well-fitting lids or tops to resist spillage if knocked over. There are specific standards available for containers and packagings to comply with transport legislation. Containers need to be of an appropriate UN Performance Tested type. Such containers are suitable also for storage conditions.

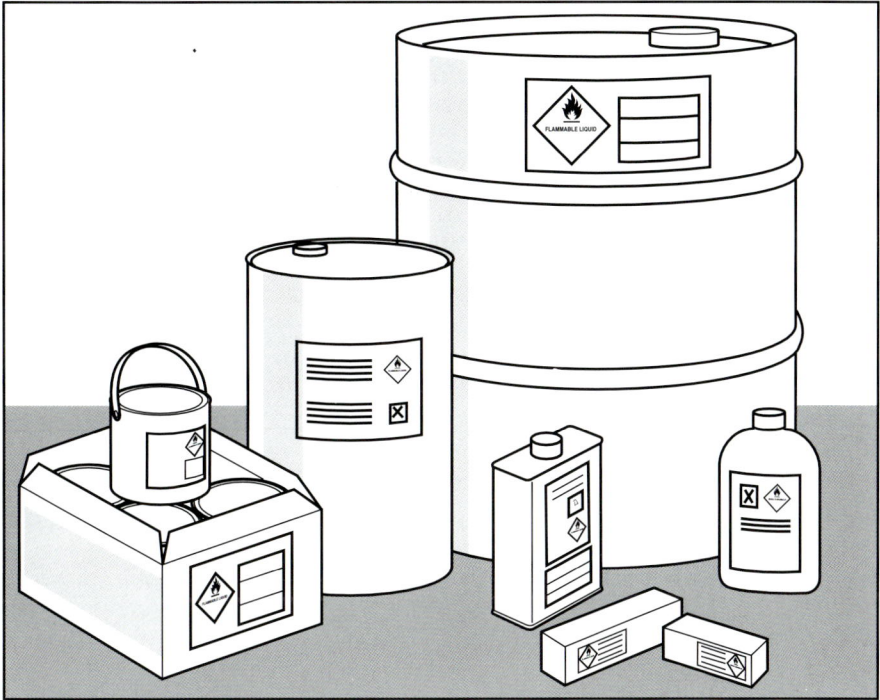

Figure 7 Various types of containers

88   If glass or other fragile containers are used, the packaging should include protection against impact damage, and may also include absorbent material to help contain the contents if a breakage occurs.

89   Where necessary containers may need protection against corrosion, for example by painting. In particular, plastic containers can suffer degradation by light, but this can be reduced by suitable shading.

90   The material, from which the containers are made, needs to be compatible with the chemical and physical properties of the liquid to ensure that no interaction occurs which might cause leakage.

Handling

91   You need to stack your containers in a safe manner which facilitates handling operations (see Figure 8). The stack design should allow any leaking container to be quickly spotted, easily removed and appropriately dealt with.

92   It is recommended that 205 litre metal drums and similar containers are stacked no more than three high, and preferably on pallets or suitably designed

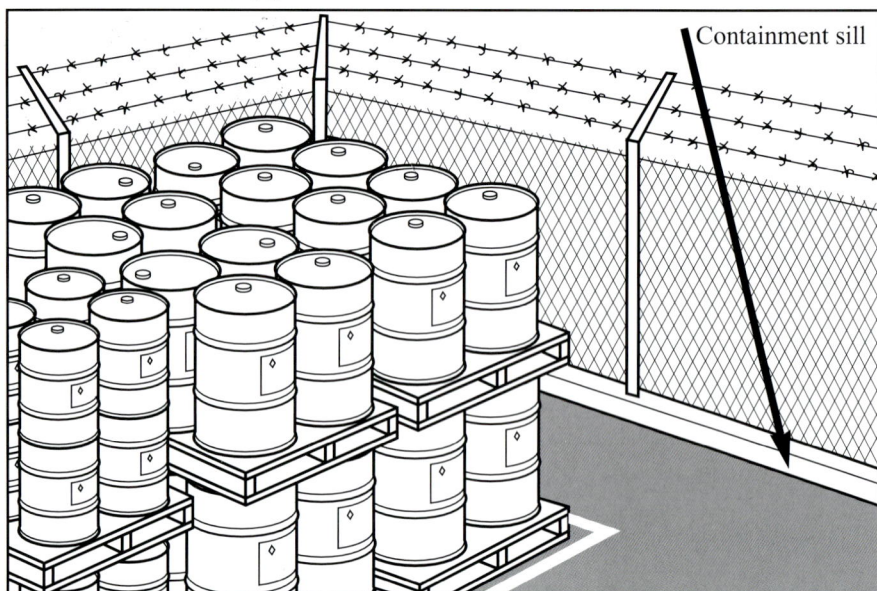

Figure 8 Outdoor drum storage

racking systems. You need to seek advice from the supplier as to relevant stack designs for other types of containers, for example those made from glass or plastic. You can prevent drums from moving, if they are stored on their sides, by using suitable chocks.

93   You should not stack containers so as to obstruct ventilation openings or means of escape in case of fire.

Operations

94   The store should not generally be used for activities where spillages are most likely, for example dispensing, mixing and repacking. Such operations should be carried out in a separate area, and in a way which reduces spills and dangerous releases of flammable liquids.

95   Further guidance on the use and handling of flammable liquids is given in the HSE publication HSG140[29].

96   Where a substance is likely to degrade during storage, you should ask your supplier about things like:

(a)   the possible hazardous effects of such degradation;

(b)   the remedial action to be taken;

(c)   the recommended storage conditions;

(d)   maximum storage times; and

(e)   inspection frequencies.

Much of this information should be contained in the product material safety data sheet (MSDS).

97   You need to regularly inspect all stored materials to ensure that the packaging is in good condition and that there are no leaks from the containers.

Spillage control

98   It is important to have means of controlling spillages and releases within the storage area to prevent the uncontrolled spreading of flammable liquids.

99   A number of control measures are possible, and some are described in the following paragraphs. Material safety data sheets will detail any specific action to be taken for dealing with spillages. You need to have these available for all the substances stored on site.

100   The provision of non-combustible absorbent granules or other means for clearing up small spills should be considered. Remember that you will need to dispose of used contaminated granules safely and appropriately.

101   One known cause of spillage from containers is by overfilling and the subsequent liquid expansion caused, for example, by the containers being stored in direct sunlight. Such expansion may also be caused if containers are stored close to transparent roof lights in buildings. Allowing adequate ullage space for the liquid expansion in the container will prevent this. More specific standards for ullage space are required under the transport legislation. In these cases the receptacle should not be filled so as to become liquid full at a temperature of 50°C.

102   Shading from direct sunlight is not normally necessary unless the material stored is unstable, or exceptionally if adequate ullage space is not provided. Any shading or weather protection which is considered necessary needs to take the form of a light non-combustible roof structure with open sides. Such structures will not add to the fire risk, and should not restrict ventilation around the containers.

103   Outdoor storage areas may be provided with an impervious sill or low bund, which needs to enclose a volume that is at least 110% of the capacity of the largest container. You may need to provide ramps over the sill to allow for the access of fork-lift trucks, pallet trucks etc into the storage area.

104 Slightly sloping the surface of the storage area will allow any liquid spilt from containers to flow away from the containers to a safe place, such as an evaporation area (either within the storage area or separated from it), or via drainage to a remote sump, interceptor or separator. Good drainage of any collected surface rain water away from the containers will reduce the likelihood of corrosion of the base of the containers, with subsequent potential leakage of the contents.

105 In the case of storage rooms or buildings, the floors need to be constructed of materials that are resistant to and compatible with the liquids stored. You can provide containment of any leaks or releases from containers within the store by sloping the floor away from the door, or by constructing a sill across the door opening. The size of the sill needs to provide containment of 110% of the capacity of the largest container stored. Typically, such sills are about 150 mm high. Again, you might require ramps over the sill to allow access for wheeled trolleys etc.

Security

106 Physical control measures allow the risks of fire or explosion to be minimised, but these can be defeated if trespassing or tampering, whether deliberate or otherwise, is allowed to take place. So your security arrangements, both during the working day and outside normal hours, need to take into account the possibility of arson and vandalism.

107 The standard of security required will depend, among other factors, on the consequences of a major fire. Intruder alarms, security patrols etc may be considered appropriate, but you should not forget other simple precautions which may be taken, such as maintaining fences and external walls. Suitable fencing for flammable liquid stores include welded mesh and chain link fencing, as neither obstruct ventilation. Where security fencing is installed around the storage area, its design needs to take full account of the general fire precautions required (see paragraphs 138-141).

108 Specific fencing around the storage area may not be required if it is within secure premises. You need to consider whether access to the store by unauthorised people during the working day is acceptable. One way of achieving this is to keep the area locked with access to the keys being restricted to authorised people.

Exchange

109 The most obvious way to reduce or eliminate the risks of fire or explosion is not to store flammable liquids. The first step in your risk assessment would be to consider the substitution by a less hazardous or non-hazardous alternative. This may however pose different risks, for example to the environment or to human health.

Separation

Introduction

110 It is recommended that flammable liquids are stored well away from other processes and general storage areas. This is best achieved by a physical distance, but alternatively a physical barrier such as a wall or partition can be used.

111 If containers of flammable liquid are stored near other combustible, flammable, toxic, corrosive or oxidising materials, or cylinders of compressed gases, an assessment of the relative hazards needs to be carried out. The intensity of a fire, or its rate of growth, may be increased if incompatible materials are stored together, for example flammable liquids with oxidising agents. Similarly a fire involving flammable liquids may spread and involve non-combustible substances, for example toxic materials, which could then be widely dispersed.

112 To prevent this type of knock-on effect, separation or segregation is necessary. Guidance is available for these situations in an HSE guidance booklet[30].

Outdoor storage

113 If containers are stored in the open air you need to locate them (see Figure 9):

    (a)   in a well-ventilated area; and

    (b)   away from sources of ignition.

114 The location needs to be designed to minimise the effect of:

    (a)   heat on the containers from a fire within the premises or outside the premises' boundary; and

    (b)   a fire within the store on buildings, plant and people inside or outside the premises.

115 Minimising the effect of heat is best achieved by distance. Containers should be stored within a clearly defined area on an impervious surface, for example a concrete pad.

116 The recommended minimum separation distances shown in Table 1 are dependant on the quantity of flammable liquid stored. The distances are based on what is considered to be good practice and have been widely accepted by industry. Although these distances may not provide complete protection to people or structures from a fire in the flammable liquid storage area, they should allow time during a developing fire for people to evacuate to a place of safety.

Table 1 Minimum separation distances

Quantity stored *litres*	Distance from occupied building, boundary, process unit, flammable liquid storage tank or fixed ignition source *metres*
Up to 1 000	2
1 000 - 100 000	4
Above 100 000	7.5

Notes
1   The maximum stack size should be 300 000 litres, with at least 4 metres between stacks.
2   Containers should not be stored within the bund of a fixed flammable liquid storage tank or within 1 metre of the tank bund wall.

117 Your risk assessment may highlight problems, for example with the local water supply. Alternatively the site may be remote from sources of help (such as the fire authority), or is close to process plant. In such cases, you need to consider increasing the minimum separation distances quoted, particularly if the fire could spread to neighbouring buildings or plant. Another solution is to take additional protective measures.

118 Additional protective measures can be passive, such as a fire wall, or they can be active, such as water deluge systems, for example sprinklers or monitors. Where such features are installed, a reduction in the minimum separation distances quoted above may be justified. In such cases, early consultation with the enforcing authority and fire authority is recommended.

Separation by a fire wall

119 A fire wall is an imperforate wall, screen or partition providing at least 30 minutes fire resistance. It protects containers of flammable liquid from the effects of radiated heat from a nearby fire. A fire wall can also ensure an adequate dispersion distance from buildings, boundaries, sources of ignition etc for flammable liquid or vapour leaking from any container. Concrete, masonry or brick construction is preferred.

Figure 9 General layout of external storage area

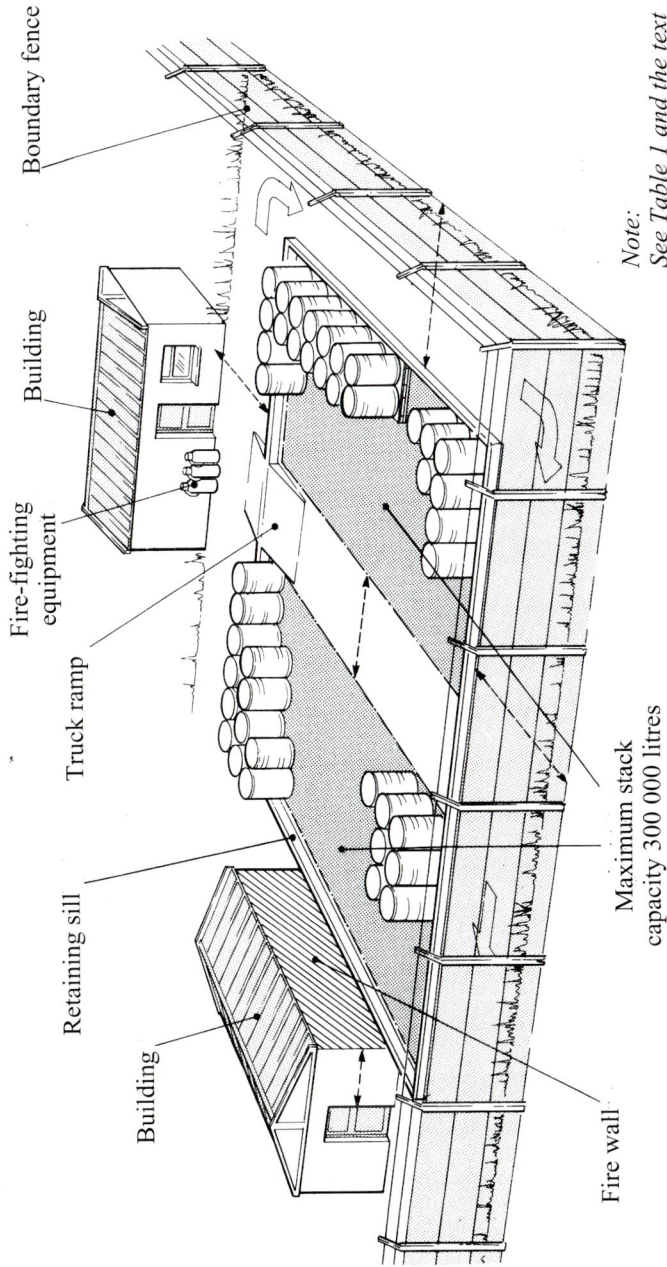

Boundary fence

Building

Fire-fighting equipment

Truck ramp

Retaining sill

Building

Fire wall

Maximum stack capacity 300 000 litres

Note:
See Table 1 and the text
for minimum distances
shown by dashed arrows

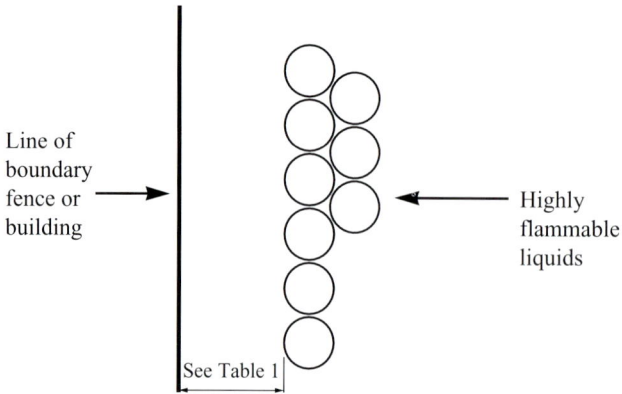

(a)   Separation distance without a fire wall

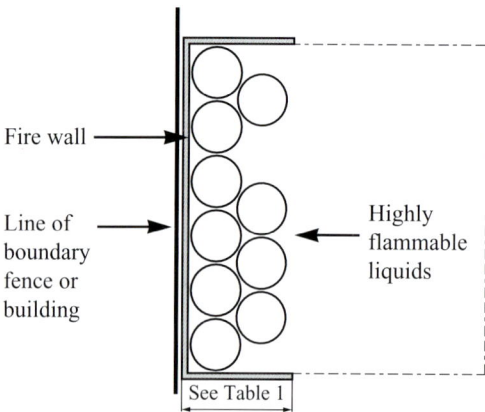

Fire wall

Line of
boundary
fence or
building

Highly
flammable
liquids

See Table 1

(b)   Separation distance with a fire wall

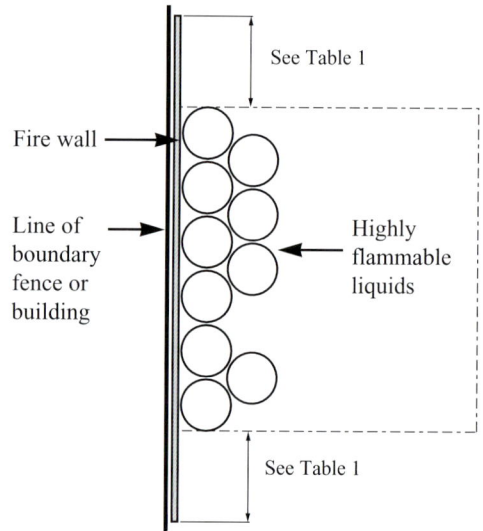

(c)   Separation distance with a fire wall -
      alternative arrangement

Figure 10   Separation distances for highly flammable liquids in drums and similar
portable containers stored outside (viewed from above)

120 The fire wall needs to be at least as high as the container stack, with a minimum height of 2 metres, and should be sited within 3 metres of the stack. Provided you can achieve these conditions, the fire wall may form part of a bund wall, building wall or boundary wall. The wall needs to be long enough to ensure that the distance between the edge of the bund and any building, boundary, source of ignition etc is at least the appropriate distance quoted in Table 1, measured around the ends of the wall (see Figure 10).

121 To ensure adequate ventilation a fire wall should normally only be provided on one side of a container stack.

Storage in separate buildings

122 If flammable liquids are stored within specially designed separate buildings, the control measures necessary to minimise fire and explosion risks are largely dependent on the location of the building.

123 If the building is in a safe place, ie the distance between the outside wall of the building and any other building, boundary etc is at least that appropriate distance quoted in Table 1, the control measures are identical to those for outdoor storage, with the addition that the building should generally be of non-combustible construction.

124 It is preferable for the roof of the building to be constructed of lightweight materials. This allows the roof to act as explosion relief as it would open readily to release the effects of an explosion. Without this, the pressure associated with an explosion would be increased.

125 The use of a fire wall can also be considered for any part of a building located within the separation distances to the boundary detailed in Table 1 (see Figure 10(c)). Namely;

(a)   the wall of the building on the boundary side is a fire wall; and

(b)   **either** the walls of the building at right angles to the boundary are fire walls for at least 4 metres from the boundary, **or** the fire wall extends along the boundary for at least 4 metres beyond the store on either side.

The increased distance (4 metres) quoted above is to reduce the threat that a fire in the store would pose to adjacent buildings/structures on or off-site, and to prevent the possible spread of flammable vapours into uncontrolled areas.

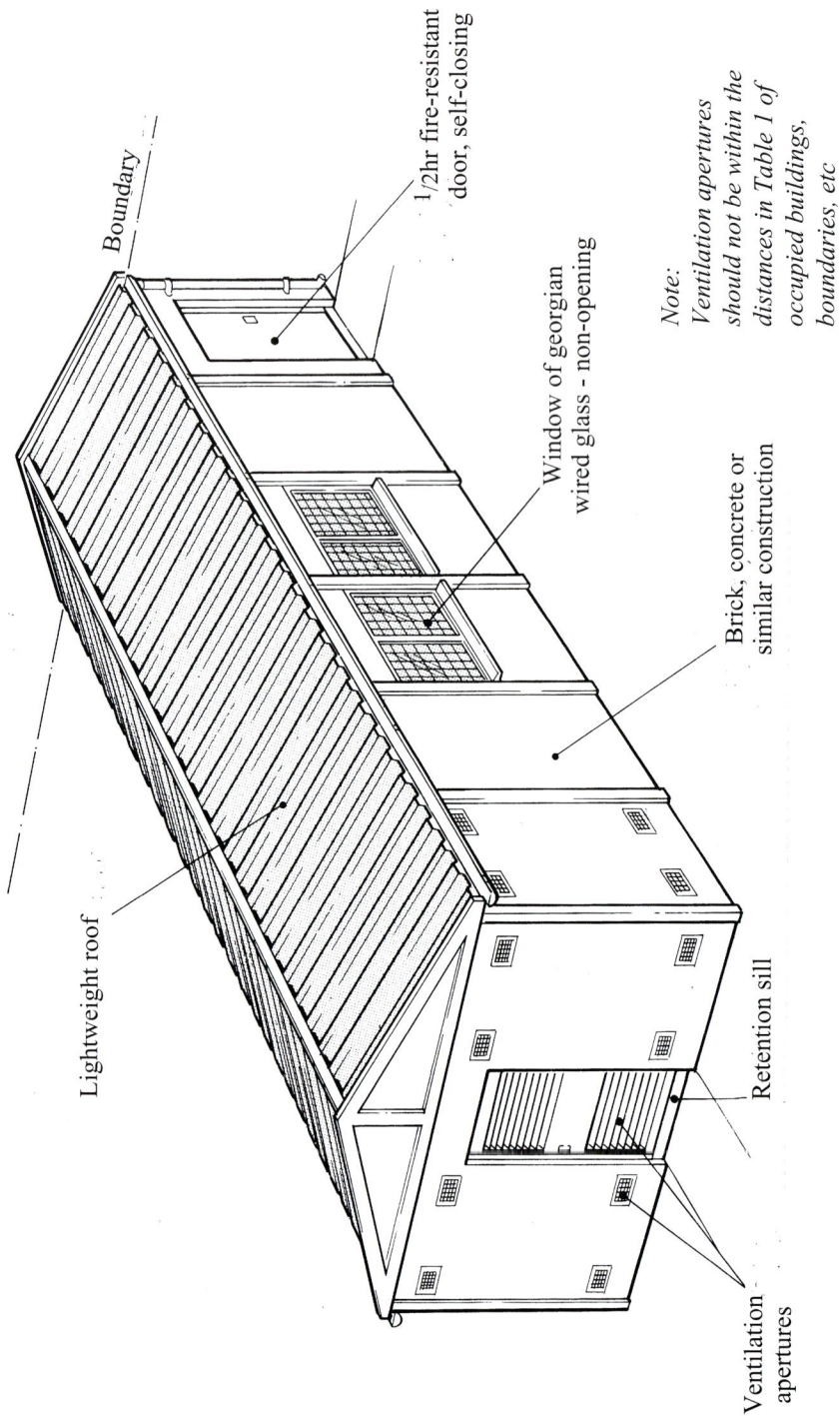

Figure 11 External storage building (fire-resisting)

Boundary

1/2hr fire-resistant door, self-closing

Window of georgian wired glass - non-opening

Brick, concrete or similar construction

Note:
Ventilation apertures should not be within the distances in Table 1 of occupied buildings, boundaries, etc

Lightweight roof

Retention sill

Ventilation apertures

126 Similar standards need to be applied for storage buildings located against the wall of an occupied building. See paragraph 61 concerning ventilation openings.

127 If the storage building cannot be located in a safe place as defined in paragraph 123, then effective separation may be achieved by constructing the store as a fire-resisting building (see Figure 11). The fire resistance needs to allow adequate time in the event of a fire to raise the alarm and evacuate the area. Constructions providing 30 minutes fire resistance are considered appropriate. These standards do not require the building to withstand a complete burn-out of the contents.

Storage in other buildings

128 The precautions for storing containers in storerooms, which form part of a building used for other purposes, are essentially a variation of the measures discussed previously for separate buildings not in a safe place (see Figure 12).

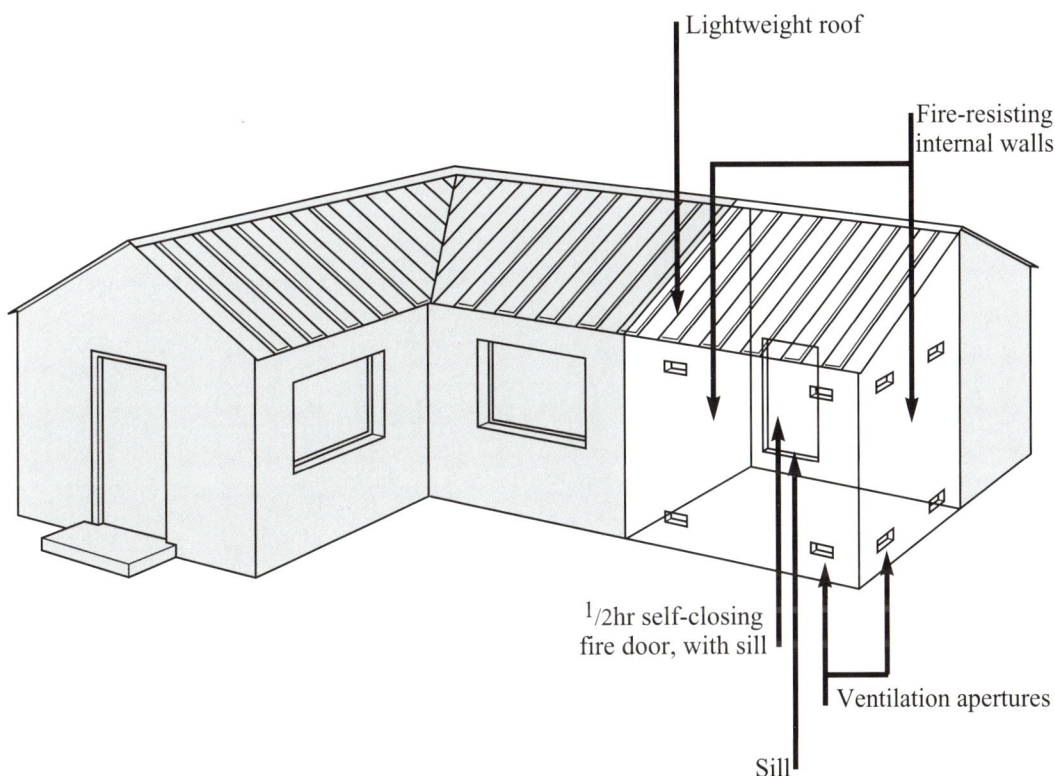

Lightweight roof

Fire-resisting internal walls

^{1}/2hr self-closing fire door, with sill

Ventilation apertures

Sill

Figure 12 An example of a suitable storeroom in a building. In the case of a multi-storey, advice should be sought from the relevant enforcing authority

129 Such stores should not be below ground, where natural ventilation is severely restricted.

130 As previously mentioned, a lightweight roof would act as explosion relief. Such a roof may be feasible for stores in single-storey buildings. Alternatively relief panels may be placed in one or more walls, provided that they vent to a safe place, so as not to injure people or damage neighbouring property. Unless the door of the store is specially strengthened, it will by default act as explosion relief. An alternative to explosion relief is to use mechanical exhaust ventilation as discussed in paragraphs 65-69.

131 In this case the mechanical ventilation needs to be designed to deal with the maximum leak anticipated, rather than the five air changes per hour which is only suitable for dispersing small leaks. Such ventilation systems need to be designed by a suitably qualified engineer after a sufficient technical evaluation.

132 Any means of escape in case of fire from any part of the building should not be jeopardised by the location of the store.

133 In addition to the standards referred to for the construction of separate storage buildings not in a safe place, the following are required:

(a)   any internal walls of the store should be of fire-resisting construction in accordance with Appendix 2;

(b)   if a common ceiling/roof structure is present between the store and the rest of the building, compartmentation needs to be provided to prevent the fire spreading to other parts of the building through the roof space. This can be achieved by providing 30 minute fire-resisting partitions either horizontally between the ceiling of the store and the roof space, or in the case of single-storey buildings, vertically in the roof space between the store and the rest of the building;

(c)   if the storeroom is in the same building as residential accommodation, compartmentation should be provided which would be capable of affording fire resistance to the same standard as the elements of construction of the residential building and not less than 60 minutes. Ideally no door should communicate between the store and the building, but if this is unavoidable then the doors need to be of the same fire resistance as the rest of the compartment and be self-closing. It is recommended that automatic fire detection is installed in the store linked to audible alarms in the residential area.

FIRE PRECAUTIONS AND EMERGENCY PROCEDURES

Fire precautions

Introduction

134 Much can be done to prevent fire, and following the advice in this book should greatly reduce the chances of it occurring. Unfortunately however the possibility of a fire always remains. It is therefore important for you to have in place a pre-planned response to such emergencies, including the appropriate actions to be taken in the event of a fire and efficient arrangements for calling the fire brigade.

General fire precautions

135 If a fire occurs people need to be able to quickly escape from its effects and reach a place of safety. The term *general fire precautions* (GFP) is used to describe the structural features and equipment provided to achieve this aim. It covers:

(a)   escape routes to fire exits;

(b)   fire-fighting equipment;

(c)   a system of giving warning in the event of fire; and

(d)   management procedures to ensure that all of the above are available and maintained, and that there is adequate training in their use.

Detailed consideration of these is outside the scope of this book. In the majority of circumstances the requirements for adequate GFPs are made under the Fire Precautions Act 1971[31] and the Fire Precautions (Workplace) Regulations 1997[32].

136 In certain specific cases where large quantities of a highly flammable liquid are stored (in excess of 4000 tonnes) or handled above its boiling point at pressures

greater than atmospheric pressure (in excess of 50 tonnes), the GFP requirements are made under the Fire Certificates (Special Premises) Regulations 1976[33].

137 Under both pieces of legislation a fire certificate will normally be issued by the relevant enforcing authority, which will specify the GFP requirements. For advice on these matters the appropriate enforcing authority should be contacted:

(a)   HSE in the case of the Fire Certificates (Special Premises) Regulations 1976[33]; and

(b)   the fire authority in the case of the Fire Precautions Act 1971[31] and the Fire Precautions (Workplace) Regulations 1997[32].

General fire precautions at outside storage areas

138 GFPs at outdoor storage facilities are now covered by the Fire Precautions (Workplace) Regulations 1997[32] and enforced by the fire authority. The following advice is provided to assist in determining the GFP requirements for these outdoor storage facilities.

139 You need to plan and control the layout of drum stacks to avoid dead-end situations, ie where escape is only possible in one direction. You need to minimise the travel distance of any which cannot be avoided. You need to make sure that the escape routes are obvious and that the gangway widths between stacks remain constant, or increase, along the route. Operational needs should ensure that the gangway widths are adequate, but wherever possible, they need to have a minimum width of 1.5 metres.

140 If the store is within a fenced security compound, at least two exits, well spaced apart, should normally be provided so that a person can turn away from the fire and find an exit. A single exit in small stores may be sufficient if the distance from any part of the store to the exit, measured around the containers, is not more than 24 metres. Exits should open outwards and be immediately openable by the person(s) making their escape.

141 Advice on the standards applicable for general fire precautions is contained in BS 5588[34].

Fire-fighting equipment

142 You will need to provide an adequate number of fire extinguishers within the storage area. Their primary purpose is to tackle incipient fires, thereby reducing the risk to people and enabling them to make their escape.

143 They need to be positioned in conspicuous locations on the escape routes, such that no one in the storage area needs to travel more than 30 metres to reach an extinguisher. Unless the location of an extinguisher is otherwise self-evident, you will need to identify its location by appropriate safety signs. Such signs should comply with the Health and Safety (Safety Signs and Signals) Regulations 1996[17] or BS 5499: Part 1[35].

144 To reduce the risk of corrosion it is sensible to keep extinguishers off the ground and provide protection against the weather.

145 Extinguishers should be to a recognised standard such as BS EN 3[36] or BS 5423 and be suitable for tackling fires involving the flammable liquids stored. BS 5423 has now been withdrawn. All new extinguishers should comply with BS EN 3[36] but existing extinguishers complying with BS 5423 are still acceptable if already in situ and remaining serviceable. The nominal size 9 kg dry powder or 9 litre foam extinguisher is recommended. Such a size of extinguisher combines ease of handling with a reasonable fire-fighting capability. You will need to make sure that anybody expected to use a fire extinguisher is properly trained.

146 You will need to provide an effective means of giving warning in case of fire in the storage area. It should be audible to all those likely to be affected by the fire. This may vary from small storage areas, where a shout of 'fire' might suffice, to larger areas where a klaxon or siren might be required. An assembly point should be identified for people evacuating from such areas, where they can be accounted for.

Emergency procedures

147 Initiating emergency procedures at the earliest stage of an incident can significantly reduce the impact on people and premises.

148 You need to draw up a procedure for dealing with fires. Consideration needs to be given to the range of possible events which take into account the following:

 (a) the nature and quantities of the flammable liquids stored;

 (b) the location of the storage facility and its design; and

 (c) the people, both on-site and off-site who may be affected.

149 Where it is likely that any incident would be confined to the storage area, or building containing the store, your emergency procedures may be limited to ensuring that everyone can safely escape from the effects of the fire, and that the fire brigade is called with minimum delay.

150 The fire brigade has duties under the Fire Services Act 1947[37] to familiarise itself with the means of access to premises and the layout, including the availability of water supplies. This is necessary for the fire brigade to be able to carry out its duties under the Act of tackling any outbreak of fire. To assist in this, you need to provide and maintain suitable access for fire-fighting personnel and their vehicles, and as necessary, to provide a convenient fire main and hydrant which should be agreed with the fire authority.

151 Where there is a possibility that a fire in the store might spread to other parts, whether on-site or off-site, you need to consider how the risk to anyone present can be reduced. You should also address how a fire can be prevented from spreading to the store if this is a possibility.

152 Clearly, the nature of the site will dictate the level of precautions, should they be needed. They could vary from housing suitable fire extinguishers or fire hose reels to tackle an incipient fire, involving vegetative undergrowth for example, to using monitors or deluge systems to apply cooling water over the container stacks.

153 You need to ensure that people expected to use the equipment are trained and practised in how to do so, without exposing themselves or others to any unnecessary risk from the fire. It is recommended that this is discussed with the fire authority.

154 The fire brigade when they arrive will assume responsibility for fire-fighting operations. It is therefore important that they are aware of the fire-fighting equipment and capability on site. This includes having in place agreed procedures with the works fire team, if there is one, to ensure that control of the incident is maintained and that nobody is exposed to unnecessary risk during handover. Any subsequent role for the works fire team should be agreed with the fire authority and detailed in your emergency procedures.

Controls for off-site risks

155 Fire water run-off may place a major strain on normal drainage facilities. Interceptors or special drainage schemes may be necessary, particularly at large installations, to minimise the risk of contaminating local water courses. Consultation with the Environment Agency (or in Scotland, the Scottish Environment Protection Agency) and the fire authority may be appropriate.

156 Guidance on this topic can be found in the HSE guidance note EH70[38] and in a document published by the Construction Industry Research and Information Association[39].

157 Where foreseeable incidents may affect people or property beyond the site boundary, the emergency services should be consulted when preparing the emergency plans.

158 Formal on-site and off-site emergency plans are required at sites subject to regulations 7 to 12 of the Control of Industrial Major Accident Hazard Regulations 1984 (CIMAH)[40] - see the HSE guidance booklet HSG25[41].

STORAGE FACILITIES

Temporary storage

159 You may need to keep containers temporarily outside of the designed storage area to aid production or processing scheduling. For example, containers may be required in or near process plant areas for use during that day or shift.

160 To ensure that the risks associated with this operation are controlled, certain measures need to be present. You should ensure that all containers are properly closed and labelled. You need to consider providing a bund around the containers if the location is such that a leak from the container could cause a hazard, for example if a leak of flammable liquid could enter the normal drainage or water systems.

161 You could store containers against a building wall if the wall is a fire wall (see paragraphs 119-121). But containers should not be stored below any opening or means of escape in case of fire, regardless of vertical distance, which would put at risk any people leaving the building or area via these means of escape. This means containers should not be stored below external stairways which are fire escapes.

162 You need to treat part-used and nominally empty containers as if they were full of liquid and return them to the permanent storage area at the end of the shift or working day.

Storage of small quantities

163 You need to ensure that only the minimum amount of flammable liquid needed to carry out your work is stored in workrooms, laboratories etc. The Highly Flammable Liquids and Liquefied Petroleum Gases Regulations 1972[3] require that no more than a maximum of 50 litres of highly flammable liquids may be stored in workrooms etc, and they must be kept in suitable cabinets or bins in designated areas away from working or processing areas (see Figure 13).

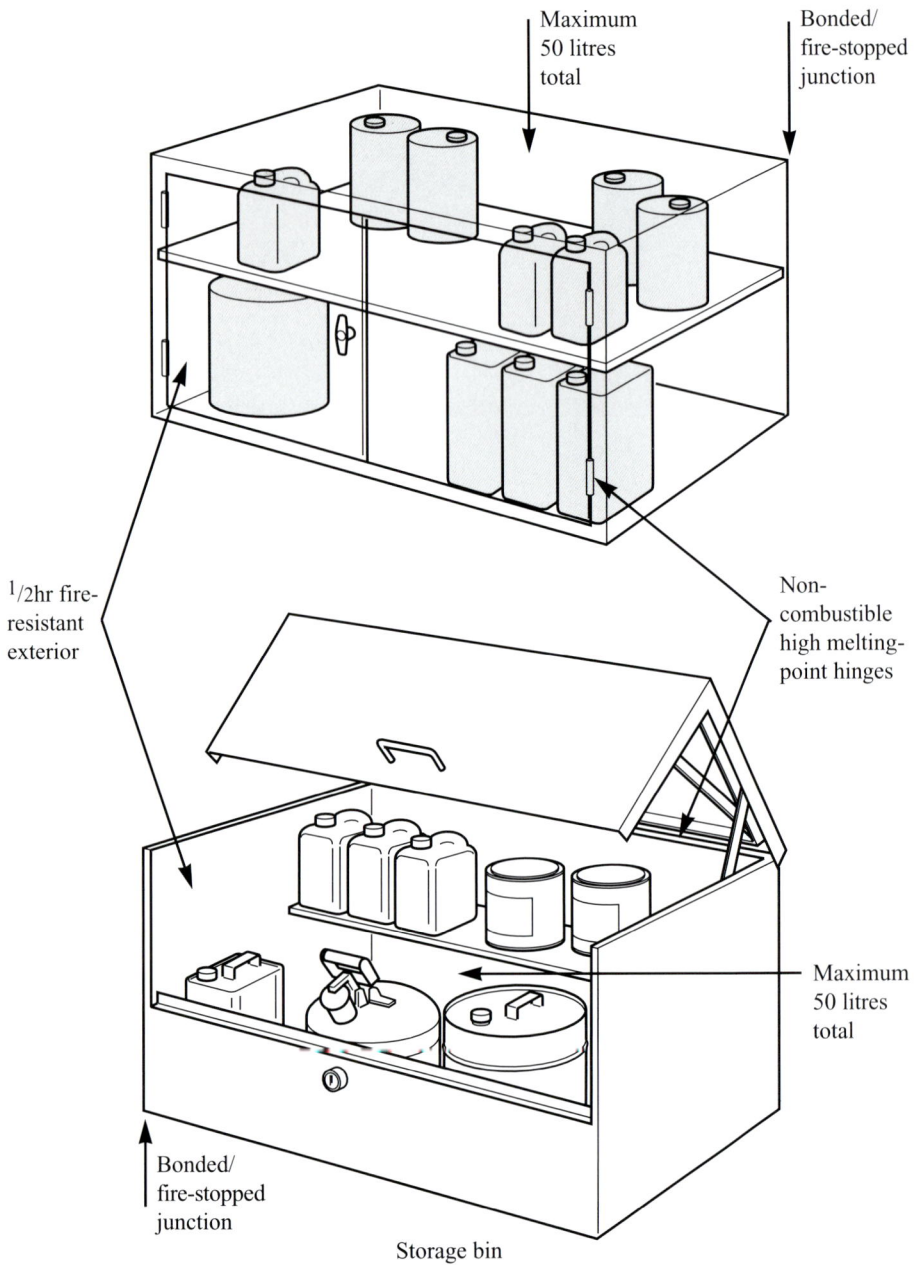

Maximum 50 litres total

Bonded/ fire-stopped junction

^{1}/2hr fire-resistant exterior

Non-combustible high melting-point hinges

Maximum 50 litres total

Bonded/ fire-stopped junction

Storage bin

Figure 13 Storage in the workroom

164 Containers which are nominally empty or are not currently needed should be returned to the appropriate store. Further advice on the design and standards of construction of cabinets and bins is contained in Appendix 2.

Storage of finished products.

165 You should always store finished products which are flammable liquids in a properly designed store. However, finished products may be stored temporarily in loading bays awaiting despatch provided that the bay is not part of a workroom. Such storage should be limited to that awaiting imminent despatch.

166 The risk associated with flammable liquids or finished products in containers of not more than 0.5 litre nominal capacity is low, because of the extent of accidental spillage from a single container. It is considered appropriate therefore that such containers may be kept in general storage with other materials at the premises of the manufacturer, distributor or retailer. In such cases however precautions must still be present to reduce the risks of fire and explosion. These include:

(a)   the store is separated from production areas by partitions of appropriate fire-resisting construction (see Appendix 2);

(b)   incompatible materials, such as peroxides and other oxidising agents, are not kept in the store;

(c)   combustible packaging materials, which are not in immediate use, are not kept in the store;

(d)   smoking is not permitted, and there is strict control over the use of naked flames in the store;

(e)   adequate ventilation is provided;

(f)   sampling or dispensing into other containers is not carried out in the store;

(g)   sealed containers are kept at least 0.5 metre from fixed electrical equipment that is not protected against igniting flammable vapour, or from heaters and other hot surfaces.

Storage and display at retail premises

167 The risks of fire and explosion associated with the storage of flammable liquids can be reduced if you can keep the amount of flammable liquid at the point

of sale to a minimum, consistent with the needs of the business. You could use dummy or empty containers for items permanently on display.

168 Full containers need to be located away from heat, sources of ignition, and other easily ignitable goods, and the stock should not obstruct the means of escape in case of fire. Smoking should not be allowed in the vicinity. You may consult the fire authority on general fire precautions.

169 You could keep additional stocks of flammable liquids intended for sale, away from the sales area to which the public have access. This could be in a storage area, room or cabinet that is designed to the standards in this book or equivalent. Access to this store needs to be limited to authorised personnel.

170 Some flammable liquids, particularly for paint mixing etc, are stored within special units which include facilities for weighing, dispensing and mixing. These units need to be sited in a well-ventilated room or area which is preferably used only for the purpose of paint mixing.

Storage of higher-flashpoint liquids

171 For liquids with a flashpoint in the range 32°C to 55°C, some of the precautions described earlier are inappropriate.

172 This is because these liquids will not normally produce a flammable atmosphere when stored at ambient temperature, ie the flashpoint is higher than normal ambient temperature. They can however produce flammable atmospheres if heated or if released as a mist or spray, and will ignite and burn readily if exposed to fire from another source.

173 In most cases the following variations will be appropriate for these liquids.

Storage locations

174 Higher-flashpoint liquids are still a fire hazard and hence need to be stored preferably according to the earlier text. However where these standards cannot be followed, such liquids may be held in general storage with other materials or in other locations where they would not be likely to be rapidly involved in any fire in the vicinity.

175 Small containers and cans etc, up to a recommended total capacity of 250 litres, can be kept in a workroom or laboratory in a fire-resisting cupboard or bin.

176 Where it is necessary to store larger quantities in a workroom, for example in drums, only the minimum quantity consistent with the needs of the operation should

be kept there. They should be stored at least 3 metres and preferably 5 metres from process activities. It is particularly important to keep sources of heat away from the storage area.

Design of stores

177 For storage rooms or buildings used to store only these liquids, a lower standard of ventilation is appropriate. A limited number of air bricks in external walls is acceptable. Explosion relief is not considered necessary.

Operations

178 Dispensing, mixing and similar operations should normally be done away from the storage area.

179 However, where the hazards associated with moving the containers appear to outweigh the fire hazard, such operations can be done in the storage area, providing that precautions are taken against spillage and adequate ventilation is provided.

Retail premises

180 Full containers may be used for display if the number is kept to a reasonable level. They need to be stacked in a safe manner, away from sources of ignition and readily combustible material (such as paper and cardboard) and in a manner which does not restrict the means of escape in case of fire for staff or customers.

181 Paint tinting systems may be used in the sales area providing the area is kept clean and well ventilated. The tinting equipment itself is normally non-combustible.

Sources of ignition

182 Provided the liquid is not heated above its flashpoint or released from the container in the form of a mist or spray, then it will not generate a hazardous area. Therefore protection of nearby electrical equipment or portable electrical equipment is not required.

183 Similarly no protection is required for vehicles being parked or used at the storage area.

Suggested storage facilities for a range of premises

Introduction

184 The following section gives examples of good arrangements for a number of different types of business to ensure safe storage of flammable liquids. The premises for which examples are given are:

(a)   storage within a workroom or laboratory;

(b)   storage in a small retail outlet or shop;

(c)   storage in a small engineering factory or motor vehicle repair shop;

(d)   storage in a large retail outlet.

While these examples can be used as a guide, your own risk assessment should form the basis for the controls you put in place.

Storage in a workroom or laboratory

185 If you work with flammable liquids in this type of location it is probable that they are contained in 2.5 litre glass bottles, small metal cans or kegs. You probably only use relatively small amounts of the flammable liquid at any one time. The overall total volume present in the room is likely to be low.

186 The Highly Flammable Liquids and Liquefied Petroleum Gases Regulations 1972[3] require that no more than a maximum of 50 litres of highly flammable liquids may be stored in the workroom under certain conditions. Not all laboratories will be subject to these Regulations but the standard is the one with which health and safety inspectors will seek compliance. Meeting the requirements will normally be sufficient to demonstrate that you have done all that is reasonably practicable to meet your general obligations under the Health and Safety at Work etc Act 1974[2].

187 Such a quantity of highly flammable liquids should be stored in closed containers and kept in a 30 minute fire-resisting bin, cabinet or cupboard fitted with the means to contain leaks from the containers. These are widely available from stockists of safety equipment.

188 One of the simplest means of storing small quantities of highly flammable liquids is to store them in a steel dustbin fitted with a close-fitting metal lid. It needs to be suitably labelled to indicate the hazard, ie the standard yellow flammability hazard triangle should be prominently displayed (see Figure 2).

189 Any quantity greater than the 50 litres should be removed from the room when not being used and stored in a properly designed store.

190 Those liquids classified as flammable only with a flashpoint in the range 32-55°C do not normally pose a fire risk, unless the liquid is heated to above its flashpoint or released as a mist or spray. They therefore do not necessarily require the same storage conditions as outlined above. However it is advised that such liquids are treated as if they were highly flammable liquids and stored within fire-resisting bins etc, since they will cause escalation of the fire if ignited.

191 Work practices, such as ensuring that containers are replaced into the bin etc when not required, will ensure that the risk of fire or explosion from the use or storage of flammable liquids is under control. Keeping a record of the contents of each bin or cupboard would enable you to quickly realise if too much highly flammable liquid was being stored in the workroom. It would also allow rarely used liquids to be removed to properly designed stores.

192 Guidance on safe practices in the use and handling of flammable liquids is given in the HSE publication HSG140[29].

Storage in a small retail outlet or shop

193 It is probable that you stock some flammable and some highly flammable liquids, for example paint and paint thinners, lacquers etc in containers of perhaps 10 litres maximum capacity. It is likely that the majority of your stock is on display to customers. The precautions detailed in paragraphs 167-170 are relevant.

194 The Highly Flammable Liquids and Liquefied Petroleum Gases Regulations 1972[3] do not apply to your premises. But as mentioned earlier, the standards required by these Regulations provide a good basis for control measures.

195 You need to ensure that your staff are aware of the presence of such flammable liquids and know the precautions necessary to avoid danger.

196 You need to inspect display stock regularly so that any leaking containers etc can be dealt with adequately. It would be good practice to display such liquids on lipped shelving so that any leaked liquid can be contained. Your staff need to be aware of the necessary practices for cleaning up leaks and spillages.

197 You need to ensure that stock is not positioned close to electrical fittings, including lighting, or heating appliances. Consideration needs to be given to the prohibition of smoking near these liquids. Remember to position the stock so it does not restrict any gangways or is close to any means of escape. The local fire authority will advise you concerning fire precautions.

Storage in a small engineering factory or motor vehicle repair shop

198 You probably store a range of flammable liquids, although the quantity of any one liquid may be relatively small. The size of the containers probably ranges from 10 or 25 litre metal cans to 205 litre metal drums.

199 A number of options are available to you to ensure safe storage conditions, dependent on your individual circumstances.

200 You probably want to store some flammable liquids in small containers, say 10 litre capacity (eg tins of paint or paint thinners, cleaning solvents), inside the workroom. The Highly Flammable Liquids and Liquefied Petroleum Gases Regulations 1972[3] require that no more than a maximum of 50 litres of highly flammable liquids may be stored in the workroom.

201 Such a quantity of highly flammable liquids should be stored in closed containers and kept in a 30 minute fire-resisting bin, cabinet or cupboard fitted with the means to contain leaks from the containers. These are widely available from stockists of safety equipment.

202 One of the simplest ways of storing small quantities of highly flammable liquids is to keep them in a steel dustbin fitted with a close-fitting lid. It needs to be suitably labelled to indicate the hazard, ie the standard yellow flammability hazard triangle should be prominently displayed (see Figure 2).

203 Larger containers should ideally be stored in the open air. If this option is chosen, the location of the storage area requires some thought. It needs to be well ventilated and away from sources of ignition. The storage area needs to be separated by distance from your boundary or other occupied buildings etc (see Table 1 and Figure 9).

204 The drums should stand on level impervious ground away from any drains etc. It is better to store the drums on a pallet as this allows easier handling by pallet truck or fork-lift truck. This also reduces the likelihood of the base of the drum becoming corroded leading to leaks of material.

205 If space is at a premium, storage of the drums against a building wall is possible, provided that certain criteria, laid down in paragraph 125, are followed.

206 Other factors concerning outdoor storage that you need to consider include:

(a)   whether the area chosen is near moving vehicles, and so will require some protection, ie bollards or fencing; and

(b)   whether site security is adequate, ie would the containers be better stored within a robust metal lockable cage.

207 If outdoor storage is not possible then there are the alternatives of storage in a separate outdoor building or an internal store, considered in detail in paragraphs 122-133.

208 A suitable separate outdoor store can be relatively cheaply obtained by modifying a freight container. The modifications would include the provision of ventilation at high and low level according to paragraph 61, and the construction of a simple sill to contain any spilt or leaked liquid.

Storage in a large retail outlet

209 It is now commonplace to find large retail outlets catering for both the trade and the general public. Many of these premises are large, single-storey warehouse buildings with high roofs. The goods are generally stacked on pallets on open racking, and the majority of the stock is actually on display. The quantity of flammable liquids on display can be extremely large, ie a few tonnes. The precautions detailed in paragraphs 167-170 are relevant.

210 While specific legislation, such as the Highly Flammable Liquids and Liquefied Petroleum Gases Regulations 1972[3], does not apply, you still have a duty under the Health and Safety at Work etc Act 1974[2] to ensure that the risks of fire and explosion are controlled. Once again the requirements in the Highly Flammable Liquids and Liquefied Petroleum Gases Regulations 1972[3] can help in deciding appropriate standards.

211 In a factory or other workplace the people present are generally aware of the hazards. They are mobile, cooperative and trained in emergency procedures etc allowing orderly evacuation in the case of fire. But in your type of establishment you need to allow for the fact that members of the general public, including children, have free access around the site, and so you need to put in place appropriate control measures.

212 You need to ensure that all staff are aware of the hazards and are trained to deal effectively and safely with leaks and spillages. Emergency procedures need to be drawn up by management, and all staff should be trained accordingly.

213 You need to assess the risks from the movement of stock. Many spillages occur when material is knocked or dropped while being moved on or off racking. You most probably restrict the public from moving within gangways while such operations are being carried out, but is your fork-lift truck suitably protected so as not to become a source of ignition for a pool of spilt paint thinners?

214 The positioning of the stock is important. Flammable stock should not be positioned close to, or beneath, electrical fittings, including lighting or heating appliances. Could you reposition your stocks of highly flammable liquids, particularly those in plastic containers, to safer locations, for example:

(a)   stored adjacent to non-combustible stock, for example building materials;

(b)   stored in specifically designed storerooms with access only to authorised staff; or

(c)   stored outside in the gardening department.

215 You need to consider whether smoking should be prohibited on the premises. Remember that the positioning of the stock should not restrict any gangways or be close to any means of escape. The local fire authority will advise you concerning general fire precautions.

216 You need to be vigilant in ensuring that:

(a)   all packaging and rubbish is removed to prevent dangers from incipient fires;

(b)   aisles and fire exits are not restricted by temporary displays or during restocking; and

(c)   the general public are prevented from causing ignition either through ignorance or intent.

APPENDIX 1
LEGAL
REQUIREMENTS

Introduction

1   It is a legal requirement under health and safety law that those responsible for work activities ensure that:

   (a)   hazards are adequately identified;

   (b)   risks are adequately assessed; and

   (c)   suitable control measures are put into practice.

2   Measures must be taken to eliminate or control the risks unless it is clear that the cost of doing so is grossly disproportionate to the level of risk. However, the ability to pay for additional control measures is not a deciding factor as to whether they are necessary.

3   Where it is not possible to remove the risk then the arrangements for managing the activity safely are particularly important. The following section outlines the main health and safety regulations applicable to the storage of flammable liquids in containers.

Carriage of Dangerous Goods (Classification, Packaging and Labelling) and Use of Transportable Pressure Receptacles Regulations 1996[16]

4   These Regulations apply to the transportation of dangerous goods by road and rail. Their aim is to reduce the risks involved in transporting such substances by requiring them to be correctly classified, packaged, and labelled.

5   They specify that dangerous goods should be carried in suitable receptacles which will not leak under normal handling. These should bear appropriate warning labels giving information on the nature of the hazards.

6   Two associated documents, the *Approved carriage list*[42] and the *Approved requirements and test methods for the classification and packaging of dangerous goods for carriage*[43] provide assistance to enable compliance with these Regulations.

7   Flammable liquids classified as dangerous goods by these Regulations are those liquids which have a flashpoint of 61°C or below, or liquids with a flashpoint above 61°C carried at temperatures above their flashpoint. Flammable liquids as defined in this guidance book will be included in the scope of these Regulations.

Carriage of Dangerous Goods by Road 1996[44] and the Carriage of Dangerous Goods by Rail Regulations 1996[45]

8   These Regulations complement the Carriage of Dangerous Goods (Classification, Packaging and Labelling) and Use of Transportable Pressure Receptacles Regulations 1996[16]. Their provisions include requirements for:

(a)   the construction of vehicles;

(b)   information to be received by operators and to be given to drivers;

(c)   the marking of vehicles; and

(d)   the loading, stowage and unloading of consignments.

9   Dangerous substances are those materials:

(a)   included in the *Approved carriage list*[42] produced in association with all the 1996 Carriage Regulations mentioned here; or

(b)   having the characteristic properties defined in Schedule 1 of the Carriage of Dangerous Goods (Classification, Packaging and Labelling) and Use of Transportable Pressure Receptacles Regulations 1996[16].

Flammable liquids as defined in this guidance book will be included in the scope of these Regulations.

Chemicals (Hazard Information and Packaging for Supply) Regulations 1994 (as amended)[5]

10   These Regulations, commonly referred to as the CHIP Regulations, contain requirements for the supply of chemicals. The Regulations require suppliers of chemicals to:

(a) classify them, ie identify their hazards;

(b) give information about the hazards to the people they supply, both in the form of labels and material safety data sheets (MSDS); and

(c) package the chemicals safely.

11 Classifying chemicals according to the CHIP Regulations requires knowledge of the physical and chemical properties, including the flashpoints of liquids, and of the health and environmental effects.

12 Chemicals are grouped into three categories of danger, according to their flashpoint:

(a) extremely flammable - those liquids with a flashpoint lower than 0°C and a boiling point lower than or equal to 35°C;

(b) highly flammable - liquids which have a flashpoint lower than 21°C but are not extremely flammable;

(c) flammable - liquids with a flashpoint equal to or greater than 21°C and less than or equal to 55°C, and which support combustion when tested in the prescribed manner at 55°C.

Flammable, highly flammable and extremely flammable liquids are all included in the scope of this guidance book.

13 The Regulations are supported by:

(a) an *Approved supply list*[46] containing agreed classifications for common substances;

(b) an approved classification and labelling guide[47];

(c) an Approved Code of Practice on material safety data sheets[48]; and

(d) by the guidance publication *CHIP 2 for everyone*[49].

Control of Industrial Major Accident Hazards Regulations 1984[40]
(as amended)

14 These Regulations, known as the CIMAH Regulations, apply at two levels to certain premises where specified quantities of particular substances are stored or used. The main aim of these Regulations is to prevent major accidents occurring;

a secondary objective is to limit the effects of any which do happen. A major accident is a major emission, fire or explosion resulting from uncontrolled developments which leads to serious danger to people or the environment.

15   The lower level requirements apply at premises where 5000 tonnes or more of highly flammable or extremely flammable liquids are involved in certain industrial activities, including storage. The upper level requirements apply where such storage exceeds 50 000 tonnes.

16   The general requirements apply at both levels and require the person in control of the industrial activity to demonstrate that the major accident hazards have been identified and that the activity is being operated safely. The additional requirements that apply at the upper level include the submission of a written safety report, preparation of an on-site emergency plan and provision of certain information for the public. The HSE publication HSR21[50] gives guidance on these Regulations.

17   The CIMAH Regulations will be replaced in early 1999 by Regulations implementing a new European Directive, the Seveso II Directive. The new Regulations will have much in common with the CIMAH Regulations and will include the storage of flammable substances.

Control of Substances Hazardous to Health Regulations 1994[14]

18   These Regulations require employers to assess the risks arising from hazardous substances at work and to decide on the measures needed to protect the health of employees. The employer is also required to take appropriate action to prevent or adequately control exposure to the hazardous substance.

19   Substances covered by these Regulations include carcinogenic substances and those which, under the Chemicals (Hazard Information and Packaging for Supply) Regulations 1994[5], are labelled as very toxic, toxic, harmful, corrosive or irritant. The Regulations also cover dusts, where present in substantial quantities, and those substances assigned occupational exposure limits.

20   Flammable liquids normally have toxic or harmful properties which bring them within the scope of these Regulations.

Dangerous Substances (Notification and Marking of Sites) Regulations 1990[18]

21   The purpose of these Regulations is to assist the fire-fighting services by the provision of advance and on-site information on sites containing large quantities of dangerous substances.

22   The Regulations apply to sites containing total quantities of 25 tonnes or more of dangerous substances. Dangerous substances include flammable liquids with a flashpoint below 55°C as defined in this guidance book. The Regulations require suitable signs to be erected at access points and at any locations specified by an inspector, and notification to be given to the appropriate fire and enforcing authorities about the presence of any dangerous substance. The HSE publication HSR29[51] gives further guidance.

Electricity at Work Regulations 1989[24]

23   These Regulations impose health and safety duties for the safe use of electricity at work. They require electrical installations and equipment to be properly constructed, maintained and fit for the purpose and environment in which they are to be used. In particular they require electrical equipment which is exposed (or reasonably expected to be exposed) to any flammable or explosive substance, including flammable vapours or gases, to be constructed or protected so as to prevent danger. Advice is available in the HSE publication HSR25[52].

Equipment and Protective Systems Intended for Use in Potentially Explosive Atmospheres Regulations 1996[27]

24   These Regulations are aimed at manufacturers and suppliers. They apply to equipment, protective systems, safety devices, controlling devices, regulating devices and components for use in potentially explosive atmospheres.

25   They require that the equipment be safe, that it meets the essential health and safety requirements, has undergone an appropriate conformity assessment and is affixed with CE marking. There is a lengthy transitional period until 30 June 2003. Manufacturers can, in the meantime, continue to ensure their equipment is safe by other means.

Factories Act 1961[53]

26   The Act defines a 'factory' and contains many general and detailed provisions relating to work activities in factories.

27   Section 31(3) contains specific requirements relating to the opening of plant that contains any explosive or inflammable gas or vapour under pressure, and section 31(4) contains specific requirements relating to the application of heat to plant that has contained any explosive or inflammable substance. 'Inflammable' means able to burn with a flame and 'flammable' is generally taken to have the same meaning as 'inflammable'. Inflammable substances and vapours will include flammable liquids and their vapours as defined in this guidance book.

Fire Certificates (Special Premises) Regulations 1976[33]

28   These Regulations apply at premises where certain quantities of hazardous materials are processed, used or stored.

29   For flammable liquids they apply at premises where there is a total of more than 4000 tonnes of any highly flammable liquid (as defined in the Highly Flammable Liquids and Liquefied Petroleum Gases Regulations 1972[3]) or more than 50 tonnes of any highly flammable liquid held under pressure greater than atmospheric pressure and at a temperature above its boiling point.

30   Where these Regulations apply they take the place of the Fire Precautions Act 1971[31] and designate HSE as the enforcing authority for matters relating to general fire precautions. Further guidance on general fire precautions for premises subject to these Regulations is available from HSE[54].

Fire Precautions Act 1971[31]

31   This Act controls what have become known as the 'general fire precautions', covering the means of escape in case of fire, the means for ensuring the means of escape can be used safely and effectively, the means for fighting fires, and the means for giving warning in the case of fire, and the training of staff in fire safety.

32   The Act allows the presence of flammable liquids to be taken into account when considering general fire precautions. The Act is enforced by the fire authorities and further guidance can be found in a Home Office publication[55].

Fire Precautions (Workplace) Regulations 1997[32]

33   These Regulations require employers to safeguard the safety of employees in case of fire, including the general fire precautions. They require the employer to plan measures to fight fire, to nominate employees to implement the planned measures, and to train them and provide them with suitable equipment. They also require contacts to be made with the external emergency services, particularly as regards rescue work and fire fighting.

34   The Regulations are enforced by the fire authorities and apply to all workplaces as defined in the Health and Safety at Work etc Act 1974[2], unless they are specifically mentioned in the 1997 Regulations[32] as an 'excepted workplace'.

35   Before these Regulations came into force, outdoor storage areas for flammable liquids were not necessarily covered by existing fire precaution legislation, ie the Fire Precautions Act 1971[31] and the Fire Certificates (Special Premises) Regulations 1976[33]. In such circumstances the requirement for adequate general fire

precautions came under the Health and Safety at Work etc Act 1974[2] and were enforced by HSE or local authorities.

Fire Services Act 1947[37]

36 The purpose of the Act is to ensure the provision of an efficient UK wide emergency service. It details the requirements for the structure of the service, the duties and powers of fire authorities and measures to secure the availability of an adequate water supply in the event of fire.

Health and Safety at Work etc Act 1974[2]

37 This Act is concerned with the health, safety and welfare of people at work, and with protecting those who are not at work (members of the public etc) from risks to their health and safety arising from work activities. The Act and its relevant statutory provisions cover the storage and use of explosives and highly flammable or otherwise dangerous substances. The general duties in sections 2 to 4 and 6 to 8 of the Act apply to all work activities covered by this guidance book.

38 The Act is enforced either by HSE or by local authorities depending on the type of premises as determined by the Health and Safety (Enforcing Authority) Regulations 1989[56].

Health and Safety (Safety Signs and Signals) Regulations 1996[17]

39 These Regulations bring into force the EC Safety Signs Directive (92/58/EEC) on the provision and use of safety signs at work. They cover various means of communicating health and safety information. They require employers to provide specific safety signs whenever there is a risk that has not been avoided or controlled by other means, for example by engineering controls and safe systems of work.

40 They apply to all places and activities where people are employed, but exclude signs and labels used in connection with the supply of substances, products and equipment or the transport of dangerous goods. Guidance on these Regulations is available in an HSE publication[57].

Highly Flammable Liquids and Liquefied Petroleum Gases Regulations 1972[3]

41 These Regulations apply when liquids which have a flashpoint of less than 32°C and which support combustion (when tested in the prescribed manner) are present at premises subject to the Factories Act 1961[53].

42 The Regulations include provisions for these highly flammable liquids relating to:

(a)   precautions to be taken during storage;

(b)   precautions to be taken against spills and leaks;

(c)   controls for sources of ignition in areas where accumulations of vapours may occur;

(d)   means to prevent the escape of vapours;

(e)   dispersal of dangerous concentrations of vapours; and

(f)   controls on smoking.

Management of Health and Safety at Work Regulations 1992[1]

43 These Regulations require employers and the self-employed to assess the risks to workers and others who may be affected by their undertakings, so that they can decide what measures need to be taken to comply with health and safety law.

44 These Regulations go on to require you to implement appropriate arrangements for managing health and safety. Health surveillance (where appropriate), emergency planning, and the provision of information and training are also included. An Approved Code of Practice[22] gives guidance on these Regulations.

Notification of Installations Handling Hazardous Substances Regulations 1982[58]

45 These Regulations, known as the NIHHS Regulations, require premises with specified quantities of particular substances, such as 10 000 tonnes or more of flammable liquids with a flashpoint of less than 21°C, to be notified to HSE.

46 Following the Planning (Hazardous Substances) Act 1990[59] and Regulations 1992[60], the presence of NIHHS Schedule 1 substances and quantities, together with some from CIMAH Schedule 3[40], on, over or under land requires consent from hazardous substances authorities. Similar provisions also apply in Scotland.

Provision and Use of Work Equipment Regulations 1992[61] (to be replaced by the Provision and Use of Work Equipment Regulations 1998).

47 These Regulations aim to ensure the provision of safe work equipment and its safe use. They include general duties covering the selection of suitable equipment, maintenance, information, instructions and training, and they also address the need for equipment to be able to control selected hazards.

48 Regulation 12 is particularly relevant to equipment associated with flammable liquids. It requires employers to ensure that people using work equipment are not exposed to hazards arising from:

(a)   equipment catching fire or overheating;

(b)   the unintended or premature discharge of any liquid or vapour; or

(c)   the unintended or premature explosion of the work equipment or any substance used or stored in it.

APPENDIX 2
FIRE-RESISTING
STRUCTURES

1   HM Chief Inspector of Factories has issued Certificate of Approval No 1 for storerooms, process cabinets or enclosures, workrooms, cupboards, bins, ducts and casings, which are required to be fire-resisting under the Highly Flammable Liquids and Liquefied Petroleum Gases Regulations 1972[3]. The main requirements for cabinets, enclosures, storerooms, ducts and casings are summarised below. These should form the basis for construction of fire-resisting enclosures, whether or not the specific Regulations apply.

2   **Cupboards, bins, cabinets and similar enclosures**

The materials used to construct each side, top, floor, door and lid should:

(a)   if tested in accordance with BS 476[62] Parts 20 and 22 (or previously Part 8) be capable of satisfying the integrity requirement of that test for at least 30 minutes;

(b)   provide an internal surface to the enclosure with a surface spread of flame and heat release classification of Class 0 (as defined in Approved Document B[63] issued in connection with the Building Regulations 1991[64]);

(c)   be fastened together in such a manner, using fastenings (including any hinges) that are of high melting point (in excess of 750°C), that·

(i)   the entire enclosure, if tested in accordance with BS 476[62] Parts 20 and 22 (or previously Part 8), would not come apart for at least 30 minutes;

(ii)   the joints are made, bonded or fire-stopped to prevent or retard the passage of flame and hot gases;

(iii) the structure is sufficiently robust that its integrity will not be impaired by any reasonably foreseeable accidental impact;.

(d)   be sufficiently durable that if coated with residues from any spillages, that these can be removed without impairing the structure's fire resistance.

3   Storerooms

The following requirements do not apply to external doors, external windows and external walls, any opening provided for ventilation, or any tops or ceilings of single-storey buildings and top-floor rooms, unless these components are within the separation distances to the vulnerable features previously specified (see section on Separation) and not otherwise protected:

(a)   Every enclosing element, that is to say every wall (including every door or window therein), floor (other than a floor immediately above the ground), and any ceiling plus its associated floor, should if tested in accordance with BS 476[62] Parts 20 and 22, and as appropriate Part 21 (or previously Part 8) be capable of satisfying the integrity and insulation requirements of the test, and as relevant the load-bearing capacity requirement.

(b)   The internal surfaces of all walls and ceiling/roof should be capable of achieving at least Class 1 if tested in accordance with BS 476[62] Part 7 (surface spread of flame).

(c)   Doors should be self-closing from any position.

(d)   Joints between elements of construction should be made, bonded or fire-stopped to prevent or retard the passage of flame and hot gases.

(e)   The structure should be sufficiently robust that its fire resistance will not be impaired by any reasonably foreseeable accidental impact.

(f)   The materials of construction used should be sufficiently durable that if coated with residues from any spillages, that these can be removed without impairing the storeroom's fire resistance.

4   **Ducts, trunks and casings**

(a)   Ducts, trunks and casings should be such that if tested in accordance with BS 476[62] Parts 20 and 22 (or previously Part 8) they would be capable of satisfying the integrity requirement of that test for at least 30 minutes.

(b)   They should provide an internal surface to the enclosure with a surface spread of flame and heat release classification of Class 0 (as defined in Approved Document B[63] issued in connection with the Building Regulations 1991[64]).

(c)   They should be supported and fastened in such a manner, using supports and fastenings that are of high melting point (in excess of 750°C) that:

   (i)   the structure plus its supports, if tested in accordance with BS 476[62] Parts 20 and 22 (or previously Part 8) would not collapse or come apart for at least 30 minutes;

   (ii)   the joints are made, bonded or fire-stopped to prevent or retard the passage of flame and hot gases;

   (iii)   the structure is sufficiently robust that its integrity will not be impaired by any reasonably foreseeable accidental impact.

(d)   They should be sufficiently durable that if coated with residues, that these can be removed without impairing the structure's fire resistance.

APPENDIX 3
HAZARDOUS AREA
CLASSIFICATION

1   The first approach should always be to control the storage and use of flammable materials so as to minimise the extent of any hazardous area.

2   The concept of hazardous area classification has, in the past, been used solely as the basis for selecting fixed electrical apparatus. However, it can also be used to help eliminate potential ignition sources, including portable electrical equipment, vehicles, hot surfaces, etc, from flammable atmospheres.

3   Advice on classifying hazardous areas can be found in BS EN 60079-10: 1996[65].

4   Hazardous areas are classified into three types of zone: Zone 0, Zone 1 and Zone 2, which are three-dimensional spaces in which flammable concentrations of vapours may be present.

5   The higher the zone number the lower the likelihood that a flammable vapour will exist within the zone.

6   Electrical equipment suitable for use in Zone 0 is produced to a higher specification (that is, it is less likely to produce an incendive spark on failure) than that suitable for use in Zone 1, which in turn is produced to a higher standard than that for use in Zone 2.

7   The aim is to reduce to an acceptable minimum level the probability of a flammable atmosphere coinciding with an electrical or other source of ignition. The three zones are defined as follows:

(a)   **Zone 0**

An area in which an explosive gas-air mixture is continuously present, or present for long periods.

A Zone 0 classification applies to enclosed spaces which are likely to contain a flammable vapour continuously or for long periods. Examples might include the inside of process vessels and storage containers. It may also apply in the immediate vicinity of exposed liquid surfaces and during continuous releases of flammable material.

(b)   **Zone 1**

An area in which an explosive gas-air mixture is likely to occur in normal operation.

A Zone 1 classification may be appropriate if either of the following apply:

(i)   The area contains plant which may, in normal operation, release sufficient flammable material to create a hazard.

(ii)   The area fulfils the requirements for Zone 2 but the ventilation or drainage is inadequate for ensuring that a flammable atmosphere is quickly dispersed. This is likely to apply to pits, trenches and similar depressions in the case of heavier-than-air vapours and to enclosed roof spaces for lighter-than-air vapours.

(c)   **Zone 2**

An area in which an explosive gas-air mixture is not likely to occur in normal operation, and if it does occur, will exist only for a short time.

A Zone 2 classification can be applied if all of the following are satisfied:

(i)   In normal operation, there is no flammable liquid in direct contact with the surrounding atmosphere.

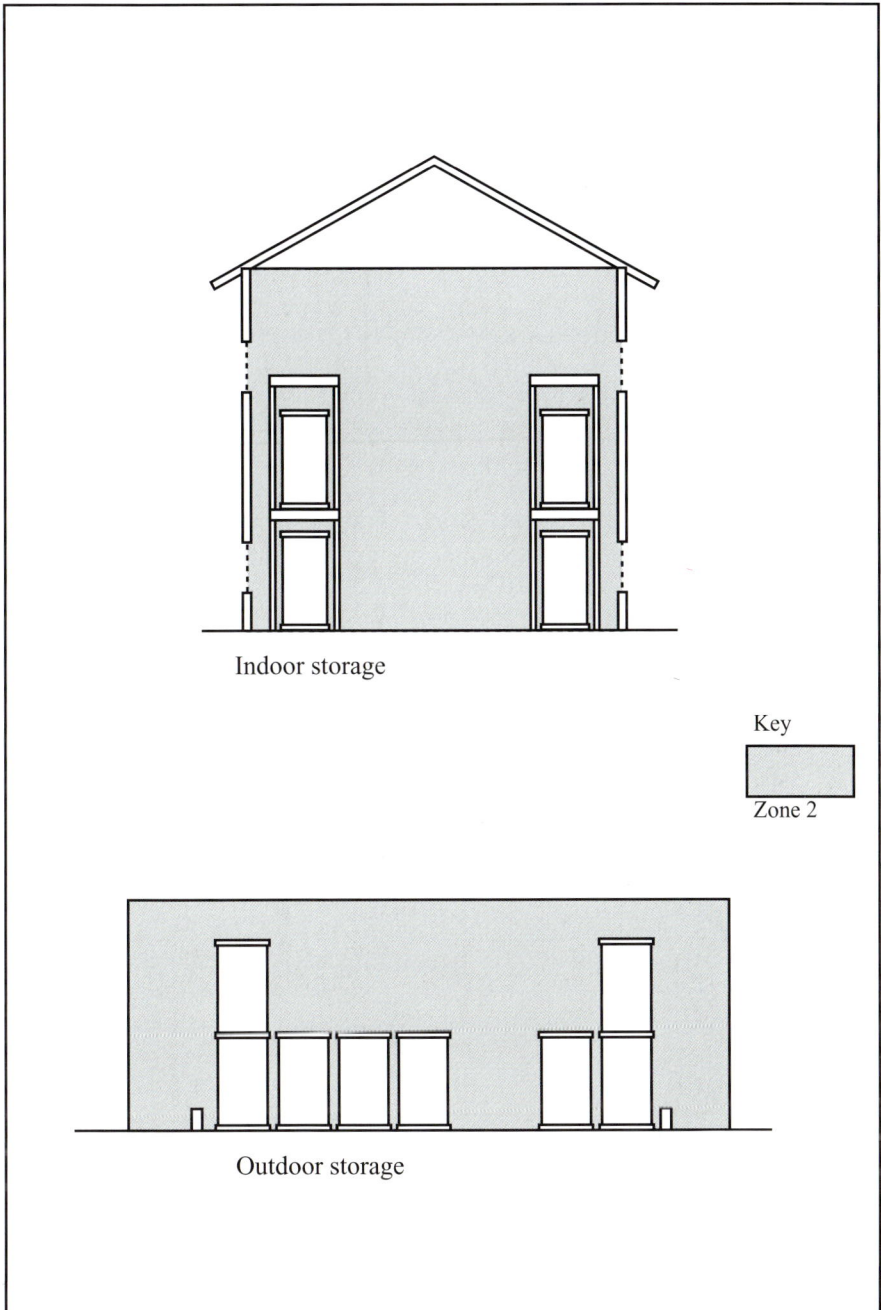

Figure 14   Typical hazardous area classification

(ii)   The plant concerned is constructed, installed and maintained so as to prevent, in normal operation, the release of sufficient flammable material to create a hazard.

(iii)   The area is well enough ventilated and drained to disperse any flammable atmosphere quickly in the event of a release, so that any contact with electrical apparatus is only for a brief period.

Areas outside of these zones are defined as non-hazardous.

8   It is good practice to draw up a plan which shows the extent of each zone. This will vary with the layout of the building, the design of the plant, ventilation and the type of materials handled.

9   Further advice is available in industry codes, BS EN 60079-10: 1996[65] and the Institute of Petroleum area classification code[66].

10   Table 2 below describes a typical area classification for containers holding liquids with a flashpoint less than 32°C. The table gives general guidance only, as local conditions (particularly with regard to ventilation conditions) should always be taken into account when carrying out a classification exercise.

Table 2 Typical area classification for containers holding liquids with a flashpoint less than 32°C

Item	Extent of area	Classification
Storerooms and buildings	Every part*	Zone 2
Cupboards and bins	Every part	Zone 2
Open-air storage areas	Vertically to 1 m above top of highest container, and horizontally to 1 m beyond bund or sill	Zone 2

*Note: For rooms and buildings which are well ventilated, areas more than 2 metres above the top of the highest container can be considered safe areas.

REFERENCES AND FURTHER READING

References

1   *Management of Health and Safety at Work Regulations 1992* SI 1992/2051 HMSO 1992 ISBN 0 11 025051 6

2   *Health and Safety at Work etc Act 1974 Ch 37* HMSO 1974 ISBN 0 10 543774 3

3   *The Highly Flammable Liquids and Liquefied Petroleum Gases Regulations 1972* SI 1972/917 HMSO 1972 ISBN 0 11 020917 6

4   *5 steps to risk assessment* INDG163 HSE Books 1994 ISBN 0 7176 0904 9

5   *The Chemicals (Hazard Information and Packaging for Supply) Regulations 1994* SI 1994/3247 HMSO 1994 ISBN 0 11 043877 9 as amended by *The Chemicals (Hazard Information and Packaging for Supply) (Amendment) Regulations 1996* SI 1996/1092 HMSO 1996 ISBN 0 11 054570 2 and *The Chemicals (Hazard Information and Packaging for Supply) (Amendment) Regulations 1997* SI 1997/1460 HMSO 1997 ISBN 0 11 063750 X

6   *Environmental Protection Act 1990* HMSO 1990 ISBN 0 10 544390 5

7   *The storage of flammable liquids in fixed tanks* HSG176 HSE Books 1998 ISBN 0 7176 1470 0

8   *The Food and Environment Protection Act 1985 Part 3 Ch 48* HMSO 1985 ISBN 0 10 544885 0

9   *The Control of Pesticides Regulations 1986* SI 1986/1510 HMSO 1986 ISBN 0 11 067510 X as amended by *The Control of Pesticides (Amendment) Regulations 1997* SI 1997/188 HMSO 1997 ISBN 0 11 063695 3

10   *The Plant Protection Products Regulations 1995* SI 1995/887 HMSO 1995 ISBN 0 11 052865 4

11   *The Plant Protection Products (Basic Conditions) Regulations 1997* SI 1997/189 HMSO 1997 ISBN 0 11 063694 5

12   *Code of Practice for suppliers of pesticides to agriculture, horticulture and forestry. Food and Environment Protection Act 1985 Part III* Ministry of Agriculture, Fisheries and Food 1990 (The Yellow Code)

13   *Guidance on storing pesticides for farmers and other professional users* AIS16 HSE Books 1996

14   *The Control of Substances Hazardous to Health Regulations 1994* SI 1994/3246 HMSO 1994 ISBN 0 11 043721 7

15   *General COSHH ACOP (Control of Substances Hazardous to Health), and Carcinogens ACOP (Control of Carcinogenic Substances) and Biological Agents ACOP (Control of Biological Agents). Control of Substances Hazardous to Health Regulations 1994. Approved Codes of Practice* L5 HSE Books 1997 ISBN 0 7176 1308 9

16   *Carriage of Dangerous Goods (Classification, Packaging and Labelling) and Use of Transportable Pressure Receptacles Regulations 1996* SI 1996/2092 HMSO 1996 ISBN 0 11 062923 X

17   *Health and Safety (Safety Signs and Signals) Regulations 1996* SI 1996/341 HMSO 1996 ISBN 0 11 054093 X

18   *Dangerous Substances (Notification and Marking of Sites) Regulations 1990* SI 1990/304 HMSO 1990 ISBN 0 11 003304 3

19   *Managing contractors: a guide for employers* HSE Books 1997 ISBN 0 7176 1196 5

20   HSC Oil Industry Advisory Committee *Guidance on permit-to-work systems in the petroleum industry* 3rd edition HSE Books 1997 ISBN 0 7176 1281 3

21   *Permit-to-work systems* INDG98 HSE Books 1997 ISBN 0 7176 1331 3

22   *Management of health and safety at work. Management of Health and Safety at Work Regulations 1992. Approved Code of Practice* L21 HSE Books 1992 ISBN 0 7176 0412 8

23   *Code of practice for ventilation principles and designing for natural ventilation* BS 5925: 1991

24   *The Electricity at Work Regulations 1989* SI 1989/635 HMSO 1989 ISBN 0 11 096635 X

25   *Electrical installations in potentially explosive gas atmospheres (other than mines)* BS EN 60079-14 (also published under the same title as International Standard IEC 79-14)

26   *Electricity and flammable substances: a short guide for small businesses* Institution of Chemical Engineers 1989 ISBN 0 85 295250 3

27   *The Equipment and Protective Systems Intended for Use in Potentially Explosive Atmospheres Regulations 1996* SI 1996/192 HMSO 1996 ISBN 0 11 053999 0

28   *Lift trucks in potentially flammable atmospheres* HSG113 HSE Books 1996 ISBN 0 7176 0706 2

29   *The safe use and handling of flammable liquids* HSG140 HSE Books 1996 ISBN 0 7176 0967 7

30   *Chemical warehousing: the storage of packaged dangerous substances* HSG71 HSE Books 1998 ISBN 0 7176 1484 0

31   *Fire Precautions Act 1971 Ch 40* HMSO 1971 ISBN 0 10 544071 X

32   *The Fire Precautions (Workplace) Regulations 1997* SI 1997/1840 HMSO 1997 ISBN 0 11 064738 6

33   *Fire Certificates (Special Premises) Regulations 1976* SI 1976/2003 HMSO 1976 ISBN 0 11 062003 8

34   *Fire precautions in the design, construction and use of buildings. Guide to fire safety codes of practice for particular premises/applications* BS 5588: Part 0 1996

35   *Fire safety signs, notices and graphic symbols. Fire safety signs* BS 5499: Part 1 1990

36   *Portable fire extinguishers* BS EN 3 (6 parts)

37   *Fire Services Act 1947 Ch 41* HMSO 1947 ISBN 0 10 850109 4

38   *The control of fire-water run-off from CIMAH sites to prevent environmental damage* EH70 HSE Books 1995 ISBN 0 7176 0990 1

39   Construction Industry Research and Information Association *Design of containment systems for the prevention of water pollution from industrial incidents* Report/IP/21 CIRIA December 1996

40   *The Control of Industrial Major Accident Hazards Regulations 1984* SI 1984/1902 HMSO 1984 ISBN 0 11 047902 5

41   *The Control of Industrial Major Accident Hazards Regulations 1984 (CIMAH). Further guidance on emergency plans* HSG25 HSE Books 1985 ISBN 0 11 883831 8

42   *Approved carriage list: information approved for the carriage of dangerous goods by road and rail other than explosives and radioactive material* L90 HSE Books 1996 ISBN 0 7176 1223 6

43   *Approved requirements and test methods for the classification and packaging of dangerous goods for carriage* L88 HSE Books 1996 ISBN 0 7176 1221 X

44   *The Carriage of Dangerous Goods by Road Regulations 1996* SI 1996/2095 HMSO 1996 ISBN 0 11 062926 4

45   *The Carriage of Dangerous Goods by Rail Regulations 1996* SI 1996/2089 HMSO 1996 ISBN 0 11 062919 1

46   *Approved supply list. Information approved for the classification and labelling of substances and preparations dangerous for supply CHIP 96* L76 HSE Books 1996 ISBN 0 7176 1116 7

47   *Approved guide to the classification and labelling of substances and preparations dangerous for supply - CHIP97* L100 HSE Books 1997 ISBN 0 7176 1366 6

48   *Safety datasheets for substances and preparations dangerous for supply. Guidance on Regulation 6 of the CHIP Regulations 1994. Approved Code of Practice* L62 HSE Books 1990 ISBN 0 7176 0859 X

49   *CHIP 2 for everyone* HSG126 HSE Books 1995 ISBN 0 7176 0857 3

50   *A guide to the Control of Industrial Major Accident Hazards Regulations 1984* HSR21 HSE Books 1990 ISBN 0 11 885579 4

51   *Notification and marking of sites. The Dangerous Substances (Notification and Marking of Sites) Regulations 1990* HSR29 HSE Books 1990 ISBN 0 11 885435 6

52   *Memorandum of guidance on the Electricity at Work Regulations 1989* HSR25 HSE Books 1989 ISBN 0 11 883963 2

53   *Factories Act 1961 Ch 34* HMSO 1961 ISBN 0 10 850027 6

54   *Guide to general fire precautions in explosives factories and magazines. Fire Certificates (Special Premises) Regulations 1976* HSE Books 1990 ISBN 0 7176 0793 3

55   *Fire Precautions Act 1971. Guide to fire precautions in existing places of work that require a fire certificate. Factories, offices, shops and railway premises* HMSO 1993 ISBN 0 11 341079 4

56   *The Health and Safety (Enforcing Authority) Regulations 1989* SI 1989/1903 HMSO 1989 ISBN 0 11 097903 6

57   *Safety signs and signals. The Health and Safety (Safety Signs and Signals) Regulations 1996. Guidance on Regulations* L64 HSE Books 1996 ISBN 0 7176 0870 0

58   *The Notification of Installations Handling Hazardous Substances Regulations 1982* SI 1982/1357 HMSO 1982 ISBN 0 11 027357 5

59   *Planning (Hazardous Substances) Act 1990* HMSO 1990 ISBN 0 10 541090 X

60   *Planning (Hazardous Substances) Regulations 1992* SI 1992/656 HMSO 1992 ISBN 0 11 023656 4

61   *The Provision and Use of Work Equipment Regulations 1992* SI 1992/2932 HMSO 1992 ISBN 0 11 025849 5 (to be replaced by the Provision and Use of Work Equipment Regulations 1998)

62   *Fire tests on building materials and structures* BS 476 (in various parts)

63   *The Buildings Regulations 1991. Fire safety: Approved Document B* HMSO 1992 ISBN 0 11 752313 5

64   *The Building Regulations 1991* SI 1991/2768 HMSO 1991 ISBN 0 11 015887 3

65   *Electrical apparatus for explosive gas atmospheres. Part 10: Classification of hazardous area* BS EN 60079-10: 1996

66   Institute of Petroleum *Area classification code for petroleum installations: model code of safe practice in the petroleum industry part 15* Wiley 1990 ISBN 0 47 192160 2 (under revision)

Further reading

Code of practice for accommodation of building services in ducts BS 8313: 1997

Code of practice for fire precautions in the chemical and allied industries BS 5908: 1990

Safety signs and colours BS 5378 (in three parts)

Code of practice for the recovery of flammable solvents Chemical Industries Association 1977

Industrial and process fire safety . Occupancy fire safety Compendium of fire safety data volume 2 Fire Protection Association 1986

Fire safety in the printing industry HSE Books 1992 ISBN 0 11 886375 4

Dispensing petrol: Assessing and controlling the risk of fire and explosion at sites where petrol is stored and dispensed as a fuel HSG146 HSE Books 1996 ISBN 0 7176 1048 9

Evaporating and other ovens HSG16 HSE Books 1981 ISBN 0 11 883433 9

Formula for health and safety: Guidance for small and medium-sized firms in the chemical industry HSG166 HSE Books 1997 ISBN 0 7176 0996 0

Health and safety in motor vehicle repair HSG67 HSE Books 1991 ISBN 0 11 885671 5

The loading and unloading of bulk flammable liquids and gases at harbours and inland waterways GS40 HSE Books 1986 ISBN 0 11 883931 4 (under revision)

Occupational exposure limits EH40/98 HSE Books 1998 ISBN 0 7176 1474 3

Safe working with flammable substances INDG227 HSE Books 1996 ISBN 0 7176 1154 X

Solvents and you INDG252 HSE Books 1997 ISBN 0 7176 1391 7

Spraying of highly flammable liquids HSG178 HSE Books 1998 ISBN 0 7176 1483 2

The cleaning and gas freeing of tanks containing flammable residues CS15 HSE Books 1997 ISBN 0 7176 1365 8

The storage and handling of organic peroxides CS21 HSE Books 1998 ISBN 0 7176 2403 X

Fire and hazardous substances Library of fire safety volume 2 Loss Prevention Council 1994 ISBN 0 902167 61 8

Guide to fire safety signs Library of fire safety volume 4 Loss Prevention Council 1996 ISBN 0 902167 87 1

Recommendations for the storage and use of flammable liquids. Part 1: General principles RC 20A Loss Prevention Council May 1997

Recommendations for the storage and use of flammable liquids. Part 2: Storage of flammable liquids in drums, cans and other containers RC 20B Loss Prevention Council May 1997

Code of practice on fire standards for new single-storey maturation storages within the Scotch whisky industry Scotch Whisky Association 1985 (known as the Red book)

The bulk storage and handling of high strength potable alcohol HSE 1990

GLOSSARY

Ambient: ambient temperature is the temperature of an immediate locality.

Auto-ignition temperature: the minimum temperature at which a material will ignite spontaneously under specified test conditions. Also referred to as the minimum ignition temperature.

Bund: the raised perimeter of an area used to contain and prevent the spreading of liquids.

Combustible: capable of burning in air when ignited.

Enforcing authority: the authority with responsibility for enforcing the Health and Safety at Work etc Act 1974[2] and other relevant statutory provisions.

Fire resistance: the ability of a material, product, assembly or structure to fulfil, for a stated period of time, the required stability against the passage of flame and hot gases, and if additionally specified, thermal insulation and/or load-bearing capacity in a standard fire resistance test. See Appendix 2.

Fire wall: an imperforate wall, screen or partition capable of affording at least 30 minutes fire resistance, if tested in accordance with BS 476[62] against the passage of flame or heat.

Flammable: capable of burning with a flame. See paragraphs 9-12 for the definition of 'flammable liquid' used in this guidance.

Flammable range: the concentration of a flammable vapour in air falling between the upper and lower explosion limits.

Flashpoint: the minimum temperature at which a liquid, under specific test conditions, gives off sufficient flammable vapour to ignite momentarily on the application of an ignition source.

Hazard: is the disposition of a thing, a condition or a situation to cause injury. The 'injury' of concern is physical injury and/or ill health to people, though this may be accompanied by harm to property and the environment.

Hazardous area: an area where flammable or explosive gas or vapour-air mixtures (often referred to as explosive gas-air mixtures) are, or may be expected to be, present in quantities which require special precautions to be taken against the risk of ignition. See Appendix 3.

Incendive: having sufficient energy to ignite a flammable mixture.

Interceptor (also known as Separator): a device installed in a surface water drainage system to separate out any immiscible solvents and thus prevent them from reaching public drains, sewers or water courses.

Lower explosion limit (LEL): the minimum concentration of vapour in air below which propagation of a flame will not occur in the presence of an ignition source. Also referred to as the lower flammable limit or lower explosive limit.

Non-combustible material: a material which:

(a)   is totally inorganic, such as concrete, fired clay, ceramic, masonry, plaster or steel/steel alloy;

(b)   if tested to BS 476[62] Part 11: 1982, does not flame nor causes any rise in temperature on either the centre (specimen) or furnace thermocouples; and

(c)   is classified as non-combustible under BS 476[62] Part 4: 1970.

Reasonably practicable: the degree of risk in a particular job or workplace needs to be balanced against the time, trouble, cost and physical difficulty of taking measures to avoid or reduce the risk. Measures must be taken to eliminate or control the risks unless it is clear that the cost of doing so is grossly disproportionate to the level of risk. However the ability to pay for additional control measures is not a deciding factor as to whether they are necessary.

Risk: is the chance of something adverse happening where 'something' refers to a particular consequence of the manifestation of a hazard.

Risk assessment: the process of identifying the hazards present in any undertaking (whether arising from work activities or other factors) and those likely to be affected by them, and of evaluating the extent of the risks involved, bearing in mind whatever precautions are already being taken.

Ullage space: the free space between the fluid level and the top of its container, to allow for expansion.

Upper explosion limit (UEL): the maximum concentration of vapour in air above which the propagation of a flame will not occur. Also referred to as the upper flammable limit or upper explosive limit.

Vapour: the gaseous phase released by evaporation from a material that is a liquid at normal temperatures and pressure.

Viscosity: the degree to which a fluid tends to resist relative motion within itself. Examples of viscous fluids are treacle and heavy fuel oils.

Zone: the classified part of a hazardous area, representing the probability of a flammable vapour (or gas) and air mixture being present. See Appendix 3.

Printed and published by the Health and Safety Executive   2/98 C100